STORY TELLING

FOR TEACHERS OF BEGINNERS AND PRIMARY CHILDREN

By
KATHERINE DUNLAP CATHER

A Textbook in the Standard Course in Teacher
Training, outlined and approved by the Sunday
School Council of Evangelical Denominations.

THIRD YEAR SPECIALIZATION SERIES

Printed for
THE TEACHER TRAINING PUBLISHING ASSOCIATION
by
THE CAXTON PRESS
NEW YORK

Printed in the United States of America

First Edition Printed September, 1921
Reprinted October, 1922

CONTENTS

EDITOR'S INTRODUCTION

SPECIALIZATION COURSES IN TEACHER TRAINING

In religious education, as in other fields of constructive endeavor, specialized training is today a badge of fitness for service. Effective leadership presupposes special training. For teachers and administrative officers in the Church school a thorough preparation and proper personal equipment have become indispensable by reason of the rapid development of the Sunday-school curriculum, which has resulted in the widespread introduction and use of graded courses, in the rapid extension of departmental organization and in greatly improved methods of teaching.

Present-day standards and courses in teacher training give evidence of a determination on the part of the religious educational forces of North America to provide an adequate training literature, that is, properly graded and sufficiently thorough courses and textbooks to meet the growing need for specialized training in this field. Popular as well as professional interest in the matter is reflected in the constantly increasing number of training institutes, community and summer training schools, and college chairs and departments of religious education. Hundreds of thousands of young people and adults, distributed among all the Protestant Evangelical churches and throughout every state and province, are engaged in serious study, in many cases including supervised practice teaching, with a view to preparing for service as leaders and teachers of religion or of increasing their efficiency in the work in which they are already engaged.

Most of these students and student teachers are pursuing some portion of the Standard Course of Teacher Training prepared in outline by the Sunday School Council of Evangelical Denominations for all the Protestant churches in the United States and Canada. This course calls for a minimum of one hundred and twenty lesson periods including in fair educational proportion the following subjects:

(a) A survey of Bible material, with special reference to the teaching values of the Bible as meeting the needs of the pupil in successive periods of his development.

(b) A study of the pupil in the varied stages of his growing life.

(c) The work and methods of the teacher.

(d) The Sunday school and its organization and management.

The course is intended to cover three years with a minimum of forty lesson periods for each year.

Following two years of more general study, provision for specialization is made in the third year, with separate studies for Administrative Officers, and for teachers of each of the following age groups: Beginners (under 6); Primary (6-8); Junior (9-11);

Intermediate (12-14); Senior (15-17); Young People (18-24) and Adults (over 24). A general course on Adolescence covering more briefly the whole period (13-24) is also provided. Thus the Third Year Specialization, of which this textbook is one unit, provides for nine separate courses of forty lesson periods each.

Which of these nine courses is to be pursued by any student or group of students will be determined by the particular place each expects to fill as teacher, supervisor or administrative officer in the Church school. Teachers of Junior pupils will study the four units devoted to the Junior Department. Teachers of young people's classes will choose between the general course on Adolescence or the course on Later Adolescence. Superintendents and general officers in the school will study the four Administrative units. Many will pursue several courses in successive years, thus adding to their specialized equipment each year. On page four of this volume will be found a complete outline of the Specialization Courses arranged by departments.

A program of intensive training as complete as that outlined by the Sunday School Council necessarily involves the preparation and publication of an equally complete series of textbooks covering no less than thirty-six separate units. Comparatively few of the denominations represented in the Sunday School Council are able independently to undertake so large a program of textbook production. It was natural, therefore, that the denominations which together had determined the general outlines of the Standard Course should likewise cooperate in the production of the required textbooks. Such cooperation, moreover, was necessary in order to command the best available talent for this important task, and in order to insure the success of the total enterprise. Thus it came about that the denominations represented in the Sunday School Council, with a few exceptions, united in the syndicate production of the entire series of Specialization units for the Third Year.

A little more than two years have been required for the selection of writers, for the careful advance coordination of their several tasks and for the actual production of the first textbooks. A substantial number of these are now available. They will be followed in rapid succession by others until the entire series for each of the nine courses is completed.

The preparation of these textbooks has proceeded under the supervision of an editorial committee representing all the cooperating denominations. The publishing arrangements have been made by a similar committee of denominational publishers likewise representing all the cooperating churches. Together the Editors, Educational Secretaries and Publishers have organized themselves into a voluntary association for the carrying out of this particular task, under the name *Teacher Training Publishing Association*. The actual publication of the separate textbook units is done by the various denominational Publishing Houses in accordance with assignments made by the Publishers' Committee of the Association. The enterprise as a whole represents one of the largest and most significant ventures which has thus far been undertaken in the field of interdenominational cooperation in religious education. The textbooks included in this series, while intended primarily for teacher-training classes in local churches and Sunday schools, are admirably suited for use in interdenominational and community classes and training schools.

This particular volume entitled *Story Telling for Teachers of Beginners and Primary Children,* is one of the five units prepared for teachers of children under nine years of age.[1] It presents clearly the underlying principles of story-telling, discusses in a comprehensive way the methods that must be used by the successful story-teller, and gives directions and inspiration for the forms of practice which are essential in acquiring the art. The illustrative stories in this course are taken from the Bible, and for that reason the lessons will be immediately helpful and permanently valuable to teachers in the church school.

For the Teacher Training Publishing Association,

HENRY H. MEYER,

Chairman Editorial Committee.

---

[1] The others are separate units for beginners and primary teachers on Methods and Child Study.

THIRD YEAR—SPECIALIZATION

Beginners and Primary Units
Nos. 1 and 3 separate for each department.

	Periods
1. Specialized Child Study (Beginners and Primary age)	10
2. Stories and Story Telling	10
3. Beginners and Primary Methods, Including Practice Teaching and Observation	20
	40

Junior Units

1. Specialized Child Study (Junior age)	10
2. Christian Conduct for Juniors	10
3. Junior Teaching Materials and Methods	10
4. Organization and Administration of the Junior Department	10
	40

Intermediate, Senior, and Young People's Units
Separate for each department.

1. Study of the Pupil	10
2. Agencies of Religious Education	10
3. Teaching Materials and Methods	10
4. Organization and Administration of the Department	10
	40

General Course on Adolescence. Same subjects as above but covering the entire period, ages 13–24, in each unit.

Adult Units

1. Psychology of Adult Life	10
2. The Religious Education of Adults	10
3. Principles of Christian Service	10
4. Organization and Administration of the Adult Department	10
	40

Administrative Units

1. Outline History of Religious Education	10
2. The Educational Task of the Local Church	10
3. The Curriculum of Religious Education	10
4. Problems of Sunday School Management	10
	40

Full information regarding any of these units will be furnished by denominational publishers on application.

CHAPTER I

WHAT STORIES REALLY ARE

The story and the child.—Not since the days of the minstrels has story-telling held so honored a place as it holds to-day, for with the advance of psychology has come a realization of its power as an educational factor, and consequently every program that has for its aim the mental, moral, or spiritual training of the child includes the art of the narrator. In the church and secular school, in the library and on the public playground, in fact, wherever the hosts of childhood are marshaled, the story has come to be regarded as a mighty ethical force, as potent as the wand of Merlin to transform good little boy and bad little boy alike into reverent and wondering listeners. By its skillful use we can create moods and call into play every response we desire to arouse. We can lead the child to love that which is beautiful and good and to dislike the baneful and malignant as certainly as we can teach him arithmetical combinations and the multiplication table. If it is true that the story has the power to mold character, to build up new standards and tear down established ones, the question naturally arises, What are stories?

The dictionary defines a story as a narration or recital of that which has occurred; a description of past events. This is a correct definition as far as it goes, but the story that sways childhood is very much more than this. To say that the wind blew yesterday and tore the roof off an abandoned barn is a recital of something which has occurred. But this bare statement of a fact would not send a group of children into a quiver of expectancy.

A story is a picture that arouses intense interest and feeling.—A story, as we use the term in literature, must have an emotional appeal. In the words of Sidney Hartland, one of the greatest authorities on fairy tales and the power of the story, it is a picture presented to the mind's eye that arouses intense interest and feeling.

That this is a more nearly adequate definition than the one of the dictionary will not be doubted by anyone who has observed the effect of a good, well-told story upon a group of children. They are utterly unconscious of what happens around them during the rendition of the tale. Throughout that period, and sometimes for a long time afterward, they are far away from the usual environment, in the country and atmosphere portrayed by the words of the narrator and mingling with the characters whose actions make the tale.

Those who recall vividly the impression made upon them during childhood by some favorite bit of folklore know this to be true, while those whose recollections are not so keen will experience in modified form what the child experiences by examining some genre painting. But it must be a picture that tells a story, one in which things are happening, and you see what is happening and realize what has happened.

An excellent subject for this experiment is Bendeman's "By the Waters of Babylon," a picture full of feeling, of beauty of line and color, and richly suggestive of event. As you study its haunting story of the exiled Jews you do not live in some drawing-room or in the alcove of an art gallery where it appeals to you from its frame. You are out in the plains of Babylon, suffering with Israel's suffering ones, who languish under the taunts and persecutions of their captors while their harps hang voiceless upon the willows. And exactly what happens to you as you view this or any other picture powerful in appeal happens to the child who listens to a story, for what the brush of the artist brings to the eye the words of the narrator bring to the ear and the inner vision. He lives the experiences of the characters portrayed as if for the moment you were one with the persecuted Jews. But he lives them more intensely, because the emotional harp of the child nature is more delicately strung than that of the adult.

A story is a series of connected scenes or pictures that make a plot.—A story is made up of several scenes or incidents. It is a series of pictures strung on a thread that makes a plot, each one of which contributes something to the action and interest of the succeeding one, until finally the action culminates in a moment of supreme interest and suspense that we call a climax. The hero is brought upon the scene, and immediately he embarks on a journey of adventure.

At once the interest of the listeners is aroused, and this interest accelerates with each move he makes until finally the thing happens that from the beginning one has hoped would or would not happen. Therefore it follows that all the events of the story must be connected. Each must be dependent upon the preceding one, and they must all merge finally into one of paramount interest. If the events are disconnected, it is not a good story, but merely a motley group of incidents. If any one of them does not contribute something toward the final dénouement, or climax, it is a poorly constructed story. It will not hold the attention because irrelevant matter in a tale weakens concentration and tends to scatter interest. In a well-constructed story no extraneous matter appears, and the child who hears a good story well told lives through every one of the experiences of its hero as fully as you live the experiences of a dream during the time it possesses you. He suffers and enjoys, he feels and thinks with the hero.

The story appeals to the emotions.—The great ethical value of the story lies in its power to touch the human heart. Interest in its characters arouses sympathy, and through this sympathy, through approval or disapproval of the actions of those who move through the tale, right is made beautiful and appealing. Wrong doing stands out in all its angularity and ugliness, and ideals are established that come only through deep responses of the emotional nature. Story tellers in Oriental lands know this very well, and consequently they regard their work as sacredly as the

Buddhist priest regards his. A lifetime of narrating and recollections of an earlier generation of narrators have taught them that stories are as air and water to the child and to the grown-up children who hear them, and in some parts of the East each public entertainer prefaces his tales with a religious chant or prayer. Hartland gives numerous instances of the religious attitude of story-tellers toward their work. Floating through books dealing with the customs of Bedouin tribes I have found a number of others. And I once heard a beggar narrator in Sicily ask the blessing of God on his work before attempting to give to a group of street children the account of Rinaldo's struggle with fiends from "Jerusalem Delivered."

The child needs to experience wholesome emotions. He must live to the uttermost now if he is to live completely and helpfully later on. He must not be regarded just as an apprentice for the adult state. One of the fallacies of the old theory of education was the belief that we must train the human plant for the future, without regard for his present enjoyment, or as to whether or not that training would permit him to live his childhood to the full. And because of this mistake many a man, having failed to experience during childhood the wholesome emotions that were rightfully his, has been unable to make the adjustment necessary for the joyful living of adult life. But twentieth-century education recognizes the fact that the child has as much right to feed his hungers and gratify his desires as has the man, and if there is any more effective means than story-telling of giving to children

the experiences that make for full and buoyant childhood, it has not yet been discovered.

Men in all walks of life and of all degrees of refinement attest to the truth of this statement. A nineteen-year old bandit, mortally wounded in a fight with officers, confessed when dying that accounts of Jesse James and the Hole-in-the-Wall gang started him on the high road to crime, because they portrayed it as an iridescent path of adventure. On the other hand, Josiah Royce, one of the most renowned and beloved philosophers America has produced, whose reverent attitude toward the Bible and all sacred things made him a power for good in the world, traced his fine spiritual feeling back to an isolated childhood, when his busy but wise mother read and told Bible stories to him and his sister. Afterward, in their play, without coaching or guidance, they acted these out as reverently as the peasants of Oberammergau and the Tyrolese valleys portray the passion and miracle plays. I remember listening with delight as that sister told how much these stories meant to them, and of the sympathy she felt for boys and girls who have been defrauded of the heritage that was theirs.

England's military chief, Lord Kitchener, cherished similar memories. This silent, undemonstrative man, who was generally supposed to be cold and unfeeling, had a fine reverence for sacred things. Upon the completion of his military course, when he emerged a lieutenant of the engineers, he asked to be sent to Palestine to make a survey of that country, because it had become fascinating land to him through twilight

times of his boyhood, when he and his brothers listened to Bible stories his mother told as they had been told to her by her father, who was a clergyman in Sussex. He followed the course of the wandering Isaac, moved over the desert spaces in the footprints of Ishmael, and up to where the multitude stood during the sermon on the mount. Time and again he read the Bible during those two years there, linking its great narratives with the hills along which they dragged the surveyor's chain, and finding in it never-ending satisfaction. And when one thinks of the reverence of this silent man for the old story times and the religious moods they awakened, he cannot help wondering what pictures must have come to him that night, when, embarking upon a voyage from which he was not to return, he went down on his Majesty's steamer Hampton with five hundred gallant seamen.

The story is dramatic.—The story that is a vital force in the child's process of development must be dramatic. The account of the windstorm that tore the roof off an abandoned barn is not a moving tale because it is not dramatic, although to the one who witnessed the occurrence it may have been highly spectacular. Therefore it is necessary for the teacher to understand what constitutes the dramatic in literature and life, and not confuse it with what is merely spectacular.

An event that does not affect the human soul is never dramatic though it may be destructive. The plunge of a locomotive from an open pier into a surging bay or ocean; the hiss of flame tongues along a

building as fire rapidly engulfs it, or a bowlder lung-
ing down a mountainside toward the bottom of a
cañon are spectacular and sometimes magnificent
sights. But they do not tug at the emotions because
they are not linked with any form of human or animal life, and therefore they are not dramatic. But if
a man is in the cabin of the engine, if a prospector's
camp lies in the path of the rock as it lunges toward
the cañon, or the holocaust holds in its grasp the life
of woman, child, or man, they become intensely
dramatic because they react upon the soul by arousing
suspense, fear, anguish, and several other emotions.

This does not mean that in order to be dramatic
an action must be violent, for some of the most dramatic stories the world knows have no suggestion of
physical risk or danger. It does mean, however, that
it must abound in conflict, in an effort of each of
two forces to overcome the other; of the fireman to
rescue orphans from the blaze, of the engineer in the
cabin to escape the icy waters of the bay, or of the
prospector to be saved from the deadly momentum of
the bowlder. Without conflict there can be no suspense, and without suspense no story can be dramatic.
But conflict may be a mental process as much as a
physical one, and for this reason many a tale in which
every character moves serenely is often so dramatic
that it grips the soul.

Conflict is the beginning of suspense. It calls the
sympathies into play. It fosters affection, prejudice,
dislike, approval or disapproval. It makes the emotional tenseness we know as suspense, and this tense-

ness keeps interest pulsating at a high pitch until it culminates in the climax. As the characters come upon the scene, if they are brought vividly before the hearer as they move in life, they attract or repel; they awaken affection, dislike, or pity; they arouse approval or disapproval, just as they do in life. This is why the story can achieve so marvelously in the spiritual life of the child. This is why, by its abundant use, we can lead him to approve or disapprove, as we would have him do.

As soon as the hero appears upon the scene, show conflict between him and some opposing force or character. But show it vividly and brightly tinged with what writers know as local color, not as a naked incident. This means that he who hears must see as he hears whether the action transpires in a glacial land, on some bare mountain or desert, or in a flowery meadow edged by the blue ripples of a summer sea. As he visions each of the characters in its proper setting the interest begins to run high. Thereafter the holding of that interest and raising it toward the climax require only that one shall move forward in a straight line and avoid diverging into bypaths as the thread of the tale is carried to a logical conclusion.

To the young child there is a highly dramatic story in Mark 10. 13-17 provided the teacher who gives it has a well-developed sense of dramatic values and knows how to bring out all its color and beauty.

On the yellow coast of Judæa by the farther side of Jordan, when the troubled were questioning Jesus and finding solace for their troubles in his marvelous words of wisdom, mothers brought their children that he might touch them; but the disciples rebuked and tried to send them away, because these adoring helpers believed he had a greater work to do.

Here enters a strong element of conflict in the desire of the parents to have their little ones blessed and kept, through the Master's touch, invulnerable to the blight of sin. And this element of conflict grows grippingly strong to the child as the twelve stand between the mothers and their desire. Suspense runs high as the little people hear and wonder, hoping they will not be sent away. And then comes a splendid climax in the moment when Jesus shows disapproval of the actions of the disciples and says, "Suffer little children to come unto me." But this lovely story, if recounted as a bare incident, if just the statement is made that one day some people brought their babies to Christ and he blessed them, will give children no conception of the tenderness and sweetness of the Man of Galilee. It will have no more gripping power and will make no deeper impression than to tell them that it rained last night and some little boys got their feet wet. In telling Bible stories, as in telling all perfectly constructed tales, the problem of the narrator lies in making the most of the dramatic situations in which they abound, and not detracting from their effectiveness by losing sight of the elements of conflict and suspense.

A sense of dramatic values seems to be born with some. To others it comes only through training and observation. But it can be cultivated, and some specific aids in securing suspense will be given in another chapter, under the heading, "The Story-Teller's Specific Preparation." Without a well-developed sense of dramatic values no one can be a successful story-teller; and without story-telling the Sunday-school teacher cannot do lastingly effective work, for the story is the corner stone in the cultural and religious life of the child.

Universality of the appeal of the story.—Human nature is much the same in all ages and regions. Men advanced upon the path of civilization forget the struggles of their primitive progenitors and lose sympathy for them. But the child of the most enlightened lives through every stage that characterized the childhood of the race. During his early years he is a wondering, reverent creature, craving the very same tales that fed his aboriginal ancestor when he was a houseless nomad, the wonder stories that fitted into his religious moods and portrayed omnipotence and spirituality in nature. So when he comes to Sunday school he is by instinct a worshipful being, and it rests with his teacher how long he is to remain so, whether the delicate tendrils already upspringing in the soul are nurtured into thrifty growths, or will die as frail plants die because of lack of sunshine and proper food elements in the soil.

STORY FOR STUDY—JACOB'S LADDER

Read the Bible story, Genesis 28. Read also the following version:

In the far-off lands of the East there was a place

that men called "the country of the wells," and in that place there was a prince whose name was Jacob. He lived in a happy home with his father and mother and big, strong brother, and could think of nothing nicer than just being there with his own dear family. But one day his father said to him, "Arise, go to the house of thy mother's father, and take thee a wife of the daughters of thy mother's brother."

Jacob knew that his father meant the Princess Rachel, for he had often heard of her sweet, beautiful face and gentle ways. She lived in "the country of the two rivers," a land many, many miles away from his loved home, and it meant that he must cross high hills and strange, lonely valleys before he could come to it.

He did not want to go so far away. He wanted to stay with his people in the place that he knew and loved so much. But because he was a good son he did as his father bade him. So he left the fair, sweet country of the wells and set out to seek the princess.

All day long he traveled, across the fields where his father's sheep were browsing and blue and yellow wild flowers were like jewels in the grass. Then the path led up to the steep hills, over sharp stones and places where it was very hard to go. Very often he stopped and looked back for a sight of his home, until by and by, as the road curved over the hills, it was hidden in the distant valley, and he could not see even the smoke that curled up from its fires.

He grew lonely and homesick. He wished he might meet somebody who would travel along with him and bear him company. But no one came. So day after day he pushed forward alone, and at night he slept by the side of the road and dreamed of home.

One evening darkness came down very quickly. Jacob chose a spot for his bed and took a stone for his pillow. Then he wrapped his cloak about him and stretched out on the hard ground.

It grew very, very dark, and now and then a night bird called from the bushes around him. Its notes made him feel more lonely than ever, and it seemed that he never had seen a blacker night. He wondered if he would ever see his home again, it seemed so far away. He felt far away from every one, even from God.

Then suddenly the place around him grew bright and shining with light. He saw a stairway that stretched from earth to sky, and upon this stairway were angels passing up and down.

"How wonderful!" he thought. And then—more wonderful still—in a gleaming light beyond the ladder God stood, and Jacob heard his voice. "Behold, I am with thee," the words came, "and will keep thee in all the places whither thou goest, and will bring thee again into this land."

It was a dream, but a beautiful, wonderful dream, and when Jacob waked out of his sleep he no longer felt lonely and forsaken.

"Surely the Lord is in this place," he said, "and I knew it not."

He took the stone he had used for a pillow and poured oil upon it and he thought, "This will help me to remember the place where God taught me not to be afraid." Then he went on his journey and was happy, for he knew God was taking care of him day and night.

At last he came to the house of his mother's father in the "country of the two rivers," and there the Princess Rachel became his wife.

This story differs from the Bible narrative, but no unwarranted fictitious details are introduced. The hero comes upon the scene in his proper setting, a prince living in "the country of the wells." By supply-

ing details that are implied the story is made as color-
ful for little people as is the Bible version to the scholar
versed in the customs and lore of the Hebrew people
and land.

An analysis of the story reveals the fact that this
account of Jacob conforms to the requirements of a
good story.

Does it arouse interest? Yes.

As soon as Jacob, the prince, and Rachel, the princess, are introduced the child wants to know about
them.

Is it a series of connected scenes or pictures, each of
which contributes something to a succeeding one, and
to the final outcome of the tale? Yes. Six successive
steps make up the plot, every one of which leads directly to the climax.

1. Jacob regretfully starts on his journey.

2. A feeling of loneliness and helplessness as night
approaches.

3. Taking a rock for a pillow. Improvising a bed.

4. The dream and the comfort it brought.

5. Dawn and the proceeding on the journey in confidence.

6. Arrival in Padan-aram and marriage to Rachel.

Has the story an emotional appeal? Yes.

The picture of the man who loves his home and
kindred but who is forced to leave them, and the feeling of loneliness and helplessness as night descends
awakens sympathy.

Is it dramatic? Is there conflict? suspense?
Yes.

Jacob's feeling of helplessness, of being far from home, from God and from all protection is overcome by the vision of the ladder. A sensation of warmth, comfort, safety, and companionship supplants one of loneliness and fear.

Is there a climax? Does the thing happen one has hoped would or would not happen?

Yes.

At last he came to the house of his mother's father in the "country of the two rivers." And there the Princess Rachel became his wife.

Every other Bible story stands the test. The account of Elijah, 1 Kings 17; of Nehemiah, Nehemiah 1; of David and Jonathan, 1 Samuel 18, 19, 20; in fact, every tale in either the Old or New Testament conforms to the requirements of a well-constructed story. The Sunday school narrator is privileged to draw from the greatest storehouse of literature the world knows, and it should be her delight to make whatever preparation is necessary to enable her to present these gems to childhood so vividly that their full luster and beauty may be seen.

THOUGHT QUESTIONS

1. Why should story-telling be given a prominent place in the Sunday school?

2. What is the difference between a story and a chronological statement of events?

3. What constitutes a plot?

4. Are tense emotional experiences as awakened by the story of value to the child? Why?

5. What is the basis of dramatic suspense in a story?

6. Why do tales that grew among primitive peoples have an appeal to the child?

7. Why is the story ranked as one of the arts?

ASSIGNMENT

Read the account of Rehoboam, 2 Chronicles 10-11, to determine if it contains all the elements of a good story.

CHAPTER II

THE STORY-TELLER'S GENERAL PREPARATION

Need of broad preparation.—If through the medium of the story we hope to give the child ideals that will be strong enough to function in behavior, the teller must give to his narration the highest degree of artistic form, and therefore his preparation should be broad. By clear visioning of scenes and a ready flow of words with which to paint those scenes upon the canvas of the eye he must have mastery of every tale he undertakes to present. But he must have vastly more than this. He should know something of the evolution of literature if he is to understand literature in its relation to life. He should have some knowledge of the origin of races, customs, arts, and religions; and he should understand in a general way the laws of beauty and how to apply them to his work.

This may seem an exaggerated statement of needs, especially if one remembers that some of the greatest narrators the world has ever known were men and women of little education, and not infrequently they were wholly illiterate. A glance at the history of the Middle Ages reveals the fact that the strolling minstrel, the minnesinger and the troubadour could neither read nor write, yet they shaped national ideals

and made and unmade kings. But how many men in
those days were minstrels and tellers of tales? A survey of the population of Italy, southern France, Ger-
many, and Ireland, where the story-telling arts reached
their finest blossoming, and where lived and wrought
those of the narrating brotherhood whose achieve-
ments gleam like the high lights of a picture, shows
that the percentage was less than one ninetieth.
These immortal but untaught teachers were men
and women supremely gifted in the art of story-telling, as Goethe and Hugo and Boccaccio were gifted,
and genius does instinctively what mediocre ability
can accomplish only through arduous training and
analytic study. Guy de Maupassant, Dickens, and
Daudet never had courses in story-writing. Tintoretto
untaught achieved a pinnacle of artistic greatness that
has been the marvel of painters ever since he wrought
with a magician's hand in Venice. And there is no
record of Adrienne Lecouvreur being trained by any
seventeenth-century Belasco. Their only masters were
life and loneliness and sometimes a broken heart, as
Schiller says. They painted, acted, or wrote as birds
sing, so naturally that even had they not given their
best effort to their work they would have achieved
more than men ordinarily endowed, because of an
overflow of artistic feeling that craved expression and
an innate sense of proportion and the laws of beauty
that amounted to a technique.

This is as true to-day as it was a century ago, or in
the yellow noontide of the Middle Ages. Only among
millions do we find a Barrie, a Lord Dunsany, a

Tagore, an Anatole France, or an Ibanez. But there are thousands of men and women who, with proper preparation, can achieve in a small way as story-tellers; who can leave an impress upon the souls of children whose lives they touch, even though their names are not embossed upon the record of the ages. And the more preparation these everyday folk give to their work, the more broadly they read and study, the richer will the background be; and only out of a rich background come that facility and fluency of expression which artistic rendition demands. It is of paramount importance that they study the laws of technique that have been deduced from the experience and performances of men and women of genius, for only through mastering these can anyone hope to come into the abandon of the artist. But above all let no Sunday-school teacher be discouraged by the thought that he is without talent for story-telling. It is written in the book of Matthew, "Out of the abundance of the heart the mouth speaketh." These words of wisdom hold superbly true in story-telling, and anyone who loves childhood can learn to tell stories appealingly and convincingly to children.

Study the great stories.—The best beginning for this technical preparation is a study of some of the great stories in the field of general literature. With the Bible narratives the Sunday-school worker will deal continually, and ultimately the effort should be concentrated upon them. But to begin with a study of the creations of the great secular writers will help one to master the laws of story structure, and there-

fore this phase of preparation should not be over-
looked. It will not only familiarize one with the principles of technique but will bring a finer appreciation
of the perfect construction of Old- and New-Testament tales, upon which all the art of the ages has
been unable to improve. Many of the pieces of literature in the general field are not suitable to give to
children, but the narrator needs to know very much
more than he tells. Consequently, it often happens
that a tale that would have a far from salutary influence upon boys and girls because of their inability to
catch its lesson stands as a model of what form in
story-telling should be.

**Fairy tales the first type of stories in the general
field to be considered.**—In this analytic study of
stories one should not overlook the fairy tales, not
modern extravaganzas such as appear from time to
time in Christmas booklets and children's magazines,
but the great racial tales collected by Grimm, Perrault,
Bechstein, and Joseph Jacobs—"Red Riding Hood,"
"Puss in Boots," "Hop o' My Thumb," "Sleeping
Beauty," and all the other favorites our childhood
knew. If the book is available, a study should be made
of the Pentamarone, first published in Italy more than
three hundred years ago, but still regarded by folk-
lorists as the best collection of fairy tales ever written.
Fairy tales may seem far afield from the work of the
Sunday-school teacher, but it must be borne in mind
that in order to tell the Bible narratives well one must
know unmistakably what constitutes a good story.
These old fairy tales, gathered from the peasantry in

different parts of the world, are told as the people told them through a long succession of generations. Therefore they are a graphic illustration of the form of narrative that appeals to the primitive mind, which is the child mind.

Works of modern masters of the short story to follow fairy tales.—Follow the study of fairy tales with the short stories of such writers as De Maupassant, Tolstoy, Stevenson, Kipling, Poe, René Bazin and Joseph Conrad. With an observation of these will come the realization that the fundamental principles of construction used by the masters of modern times are identical with those according to which the unlettered tribesman cast his narratives. Regardless of embellishment, regardless of the number of bypaths along which the characters stray as the action of the plot unfolds, the salient features of construction are ever the same. There is the immediate limning of the characters upon the film outspread to the eye in the beginning of the story. There is the conflict that makes for strong dramatic suspense. There is a series of incidents as the action moves speedily and in a direct line through the body of the story, heightening the interest with every sentence. And there is the apex of interest, a moment of intense suspense and final revealment in what we call the climax. In a folk tale from the Fiji Islands or in that beautifully finished Slavic gem of Tolstoy, "Where Love Is There Is God Also," every sentence is contributory to the action of the characters. Every incident is dependent upon or contributes to some other incident, without which the full plot of the narrative could not be revealed. In a word, a good story, whether ancient tale or modern, is as free from extraneous matter as is the refined gold of a Tiffany bracelet from the ore with which it came from the Nevada desert or from the hydraulic gulches of the Bolivian mines. Like a beautifully garbed human being, when we strip it of its trappings, the body is like that of every other human being, the society queen and the beggar in the public square, the king on a jeweled throne and the groom who cares for his horse. Realization of this fact is of paramount importance to whoever aspires to become a story-teller, for once he knows as he knows his arithmetic tables what constitutes a story, obstructions vanish from the way and success is assured.

Analysis the aim of story study.—In studying a story, the narrator must not, in his interest in the plot, lose sight of the fact that his aim is analysis. Constantly he must dissect, and as he dissects he must reflect upon the result. Otherwise the most omnivorous reading will benefit him very little in his desire to become a story-teller. If the tale is unfamiliar and grips his interest so that he loses sight of the principles of structure as he reads, let him go through it once for content, and then with an analytical mind, in conformity with the following outline:

Is there a rambling introduction?

Do the characters enter and attract attention with the first paragraph?

Does the story begin with conversation or in narrative form?

Does the plot unfoldment commence with the very first paragraph?

Does the action move in a straight line, or does it zigzag and divert interest from the main thread of the plot?

Does the tale culminate in a gripping climax, or does it seemingly get nowhere?

Is there a nonessential conclusion, or does the story end with the action?

Is there anything in the story that is nonessential, anything that might be cut away without spoiling it?

By an analytic study of stories according to the preceding outline a sense of proper narrative form will be acquired more quickly than in any other way. One student, who has made a place and name for herself in the story-telling world, upon first taking up the work said she had no talent for narration, and therefore could not hope to become a good story-teller. But a course in story-telling was a prerequisite for the playground certificate she was eager to obtain, and therefore she went into the study of the subject with much earnestness. Beginning with the fairy tales, she wrote an analysis of the form of "The Ugly Duckling," "Hop o' My Thumb," and Bechstein's "Seven at One Blow." Followed then in her notebook an analysis and comparison of De Maupassant's "Necklace," "The Gold Bug," by Edgar Allan Poe, and René Bazin's "The Man Who Brought the River." This gave her a conception of the component elements of a story that she had believed impossible for her to acquire, and which became the foundation of a successful career. Continuing this intensive study as she told many stories to children, she came into a confidence in her ability to tell stories because she knew unmistakably what constituted a good story. At the end of a year she had made so excellent a record with story hours in her playground work that she was appointed special story-teller on the five public playgrounds of her town. Yet in the beginning she said she could not tell stories, and not until an analysis of stories brought light and confidence, and much study and practice followed that analysis, was she able to do so.

Analytic study of Bible stories to follow that of tales in the general field.—Since the aim of the Sunday-school worker is to tell the Old- and New-Testament stories so skillfully that they will be vivid and convincing to the child, the study of stories in the general field is but a means to that end, a blazing of the trail that will take him to the broad highway that leads to the goal. After several fairy tales and modern short stories have been dissected, the same method of analytic study should be applied to the Bible stories.

The following list is a good one for the beginner:

The Story of the Creation—Genesis 1.

Lot Taken Captive and Rescued—Genesis 14.

The Story of Moses—Exodus 2.

The Building of the Temple—1 Kings 6.

Study of book on the technique of the short story a necessary preparation.—Hand in hand with an analysis of stories should go some book on the technique of the short story. For this an excellent work is *Writing the Short Story*, by Berg Esenwein. Whether one deals with the written or oral story the principles of construction are identical, and the very best training the narrator can have for his work is the writing of stories. Students who have been required to write one story to every two or three told in class or on the playground testify to the fact that the writing phase of the preparation has been more helpful to them than practice in telling. Once a person knows how to construct, the rendition becomes easy, and to the beginner the power to construct comes more easily through writing than through telling. *The Philosophy of the Short Story*, by Brander Matthews, is another helpful book, and if possible the narrator should familiarize himself with *The Evolution of Literature*, by A. S. MacKenzie. This is a very comprehensive story of how literature has developed from the first crude, spoken form to the highly artistic creation of Hugo or Tolstoy. And it will give a conception of the value to the race of the spoken tale that every narrator should possess.

One of the chief prerequisites for the broad preparation that makes possible big achievement in the field of story-telling is some knowledge of the science of æsthetics, of the principles and laws of beauty and their relation to the arts and to life. Since story-telling is an art, its relation to and dependence upon all the other arts should be understood clearly. The study of æsthetics will give this understanding, and through it will be seen the place of each of the arts in the universal scheme of things. Through it will come also a conception of the value to humanity of the specific one in which he is interested that will make him willing to labor to be worthy of being a toiler in its ranks. He will begin to believe with the great creator of "Parsifal," that there must be some last judgment that shall fearfully damn all those who upon this earth have dared to make profit of this chaste and holy art; who have disgraced and dishonored it through badness of heart and the coarse instincts of sensuality, or by being satisfied to give to it anything but the best fruit of soul and brain.

For a study of the broad field of æsthetics in a detailed, comprehensive way, an excellent book is *Essentials of Æsthetics,* by George Lansing. This is a fascinating presentation of the entire field of harmony, form, color, rhythm, proportion, and sound as they exist in nature and in the fine arts, and will give an understanding of what constitutes the beautiful and appealing in any art. A less technical, but illuminating and inspiring work is *The Philosophy of Art,* by Edward Howard Griggs. In this are considered the primitive sources of art, the defining forces behind the artist, the unique function of each of the fine arts, their unity and relation to each other. This last mentioned chapter will greatly aid the teller of stories to little children. Although it makes no mention of story-telling as an independent art, what is true of the drama in its appeal to the mind and heart is

true of the spoken tale, which is a form of drama.
Therefore the treatment of the drama in any book on
æsthetics has a direct bearing upon the work of the
narrator.

**A study of pictures is part of the equipment of
the story-teller.**—The teller of stories to little children must often draw from the entire field of art if
his work is to be well balanced and effective. This
fact should be fully sensed by the narrator. Consequently, it is repeated for the sake of emphasis. To
give the Bible stories without investing them with the
color of Giulio Romano, Pellafrina da Modena, Mu-
rillo, Michael Angelo, Titian, Doré or Rembrandt is
to permit the child to experience only half the delight he should have in them. Nothing so vivifies a
tale as a picture illustrating that tale, and by means
of the cheap reproductions sent out by the several
print companies, this vivifying influence is within
the reach of every Sunday school. The teacher in the
Beginners and Primary Departments will often find
in the world of art not allied with the biblical subjects
many pictures that tend to bring home to the child
the lesson the Bible story teaches. A very helpful
book for these workers is *Kindergarten Bible Stories,*
by L. E. Cragin, because of its selection of pictures,
while the stories given therein will furnish many
suggestions for other stories. The classified catalogues issued by the Brown, Perry, Prang, and Uni-
versity Print Companies are suggestive. Grouped
under the headings, "Biblical Subjects," "Italian Art,"
"French Art," etc., pictures are classified in such a

manner that even the teacher who has no knowledge
of art will be able to make a selection that will greatly
aid her in her work. When the course for the year
is outlined, if the helps furnished do not include pictures, the teacher should make a list of story themes
and study the catalogues for pictures illustrative of
each, that they may be ordered and ready for the class
when needed. A well-classified list of pictures for
the needs of workers in the various departments of
the Sunday school is also found in *The Church School,*
by Walter S. Athearn.

Whenever possible the child should have a small
picture to take home, that he may live with the story
and the more completely possess it. Miniatures may
be obtained from the print companies at the rate of
two for one cent, and these are very valuable if the
child is taught to study them in relation to the story
after he has heard it, and to see the story in the picture. Teach the children that there are different ways
of telling a story, a language way and a picture way,
and help them to see and enjoy in each picture the
story the artist had in mind when he drew it.

**A knowledge of great music part of the equip-
ment of the story-teller.**—Music will contribute as
splendidly to the work of the story-teller as painting
and scripture. This does not mean that one must be
a musician in order to be a successful narrator, but
it does mean that if his work is to be wholly effective
he must have some knowledge of the great music of
the world, so that now and then he can bring it into
his work. Those who have not had a musical edu-

cation will find that studying the catalogues of the
talking machine companies will be a tremendous help
to them. These are so well classified and cover so
completely the entire field of music that a study of
them is a foundation for a fairly broad knowledge
of the world's great melodies. One mother who had
had no musical training, but who was eager to give
her children the best, used a talking machine cata-
logue as a textbook on musical literature. Supple-
menting the outlines therein given with many references to the encyclopædia, and then armed with a
list of composers' works or musical themes, she
bought the records that would give her daughters the
knowledge and appreciation she coveted for them,
and the results in culture and spiritual training in that
family were almost past believing. Such a preparation will give the Sunday-school worker an equally
rich equipment, one that it is very necessary he should
have, for the child needs to hear great music as he
hears great stories. He will not catch the full meaning of the melodies of the masters, but he enjoys them
more than most adults realize. After telling the
story of the creation I have used with gratifying results records of Haydn's "The Heavens Are Telling"
and "With Verdure Clad." The account of Moses in
the bulrushes I always supplement with some flute,
oboe, or clarinet records, as being sounds like those
the baby heard as he lay there in the reeds. My
favorites for this story are "Song of the Shepherd
Lehl"—Rimsky-Korsakow, as sung by Alma Gluck;
"The Pipes of Pan"—Adrian Ross-Edward Elgar;

"The Wind Among the Trees"—Briccialdi; and De-
bussy's "Afternoon of a Faun"—("L'Après-Midi d'un
Faune"). Many selections that the Sunday-school
worker can use to advantage are listed in a little book
issued by the Victor Talking Machine Company,
"Pan and His Pipes." This is especially valuable
because of its classified selection of Christmas music
and crusaders' songs. Usually instrumental records
are preferable to vocal ones, because considerable
concentration is required upon the words to catch
them as they come from the machine. Consequently
little people get more pleasure and benefit out of just
losing themselves in the melody. But sometimes
quartets, trios, choruses, and solos, especially those
of Alma Gluck, Louise Homer, and de Gogorza,
whose enunciation is especially clear, are enjoyed by
children quite as much as the instrumental records.
And if a good orchestra is available, or some musician will come in to play to supplement the stories,
the teacher is fortunate indeed.

All the great oratorios can be made to contribute
toward the child's joy in the Sunday school and in
fixing the Sunday-school stories, and it is a mistake
to think we should not use them because their full
meaning is beyond the understanding of little people.
The sea is beyond their full understanding too, but
it touches their souls with a sense of its vastness in
a way that they do not forget. So too with great
melody, the mighty sacred music of the world, the
chant, chorals, and oratorios, and the compositions of
every master whose work was to him a religion.

They open the gates to the emotional crypts, the places where feelings and instincts lie, and in a vague, incomprehensible way shake the whole being with a realization of something that is great and endless. I know this out of memories of my own childhood and by the response of hundreds of children who have come under my observation. At seven years of age the superb artistry of Rossini's overture to "William Tell" was beyond my comprehension. But a story had made it clear that it was a song of herdsmen and shepherds, of mountain streams and valleys flecked with the shadows of Swiss chalets, and it brought to me—and does yet, for that matter, for the old-time pictures reoccur—the green sweetness of the forest and fairies and pipers dancing to the cadence of cataracts. And what music beyond my full understanding brought to me, it will bring to any child who has a lively emotional nature and nimble imagination, once the story has awakened them into activity.

A knowledge of primitive religious beliefs should be part of the equipment of the Sunday-school story-teller.—The Sunday-school worker who knows something of how the religious beliefs of the world have evolved and understands the religious attitude of primitive man toward the unseen forces of nature is better equipped to tell stories sympathetically to children, because the attitude of primitive man toward nature and religion is the child attitude. For this preparation there is no better book than *Myth, Ritual and Religion*, by Andrew Lang, which traces religious development from the awe of nature which characterizes the savage through every crude process to the dawn of Christianity. He touches the worshipful side of the aborigine of Asia, of the South Sea islander, and the one in the American forests when the white man came. Without knowing something of the attitude toward nature and the controlling forces of nature of these simple men one cannot fully understand the religious moods of the child.

Nature study is an essential part of the preparation of the story-teller.—Nature and religion are very closely associated in the mind of the child, as they were with primitive man and are with the present day savage. Therefore the more deeply the story-teller studies nature, the more he knows of birds and beasts, flowers, trees, and the wild, free places, the closer he comes into touch with nature's God and the more he can contribute toward the religious life of the child. It is a fixed belief with me that every worker with children, whether religious or secular, should know and know well such books as John Van Dyke's *The Desert, The Opal Sea, The Mountains,* and *The Grand Cañon of the Colorado.* Poetic in their conception, full of a sense of the presence of God although they make little mention of God, they arouse a feeling and reverence for and kinship with nature whose value to the story-teller cannot be estimated, for above all others the story-teller needs to have reverence and a feeling of kinship with nature and nature's God. A study of such books as Nora Baynes' *Wild Bird Guests,* David Starr Jordan's *Birds and Beasts,* and Fabre's marvelous works on insect life will greatly aid the Sunday-school worker. With the story of David the Shepherd should go a tale of white-fleeced lamb, of field daisy and of bird that wings toward heaven lilting blithely as it flies. These were part of the environment of the shepherd, and will make his story more vivid to the child. By the many references to nature in the Bible we know that the Hebrews lived very close to nature, and that is one reason why the Bible tales are so appealing to the child. They are in harmony with winds, sunshine, blossoms and running brooks, and so is childhood. In many, many ways bits of nature, of animal anecdote and characteristics will illuminate the work of the Sunday school teacher, sometimes in illustrating traits of character, sometimes in bringing a biblical hero close to home. Therefore a study of elementary geology, zoology, and astronomy will abundantly reward. Often objection is made to introducing science into Sunday-school work because of the danger of making children irreligious. But how can it do this if truthfully and reverently presented? The more one knows of the wonders of the universe, the more reverence he feels for the Power that fashioned them, and instead of making him less devout it tends to make him more so. One of the greatest scientists of our time is as steadfast in his belief in the Christ of Nazareth as was his mother sixty years ago, who had no education beyond that of the lower elementary grades. Not long ago, when asked his opinion about the idea so often advanced that science and religion are as the proverbial oil and water, he smiled and answered, "Suppose one does believe that life evolved from a germ; the great question is 'Who made the germ?'"

Nature and religion go so closely hand in hand that they cannot well be separated and should not be with the child. Animal stories, plant stories, stories of stones and stars—all these should supplement the Bible account of the creation. Especially do the religious animal legends mean much to the child, such narratives as "Robin Redbreast," one of the loveliest tales that ever came out of the East, which Selma Lagerlof gives in "Christ Legends." It is an exquisite piece of literature to use in connection with the Hebrew account of the dawn of life, and should be told again at Easter time, especially the part the Syrians believe the little bird played on the day of the crucifixion. The child will respond to it with every fiber of his emotional nature, will grasp the truth wrapped up in it, and will joyfully memorize the beautiful lesson, "Because of thy compassion thou hast won all thou hast been striving for ever since the world was created, thou and thy kindred."

Many another Old- and New-Testament tale can be illuminated by a nature story or legend, and, used freely, these tales will lead children to religion instead of away from it, and through them they will gain such realization of the marvels of nature that they will see with vividness the workings of God.

Especially helpful are nature stories in awakening in the little child that God-consciousness we wish to develop, and in giving him a sense of God's care for His children and for all defenseless creatures. The father and mother birds' care of their little ones, the nest-making, food-gathering and feeding are splendidly illustrative of the love and watchfulness of the Father of all. There is a great lesson in the story of the seasons—how spring, summer, autumn, and winter each brings a gift that makes for the comfort and well-being of all living things. The story of the rain and the dew, that quickens into life the brown seed; the snow that is a white mantle for the sleeping field of wheat; the flight of birds southward as cold days come and the return flying with mild weather; the hibernating of bear or woodchuck during the winter days and the coming of each from its hole with the creeping of spring across the border—all these have within them power to arouse in the child the questions, "What makes the rain and the sunshine?" "Who tells the birdie it is time to move and shows him the way?" And then how easy it is to lead that child into an understanding of God!

Plant and animal, bird and flower, river and mountain peak in story, song, and poem, all should go together in this blessed age of innocence, that it may be an age of delight to the child as well as one of abundant sowing. To sing Jessie Gaynor's sweet song, "The Wee Little Nest," or Emilie Poulsson's "Cradle Nest" after the children hear a bird story will seem to them like living with the birds and rocking in the tree beside them. For this reason such collections as *Holiday Songs*—Poulsson; *Songs and Games for Little People*—Walker and Jenks; *Song Echoes from Child Land*—Jenks and Rust; and *Song Stories for the Kindergarten*—Hill, should be in every Sunday school library.

The story-teller must have an understanding of psychology.—We must know something about the workings of the child mind and heart in order to reach them. Therefore a knowledge of psychology is absolutely essential to the story-teller. All teacher-training courses include this subject, but the isolated worker who has no contact with the school of religious education, the one who must blaze his trail unaided and get his training in solitude, will need at least one good book on psychology if he is to achieve largely. For the worker with sufficient educational foundation to assimilate a technical, philosophic work I would recommend an old, old book, perhaps the greatest ever written upon this subject, *Emile, or Education,* by Jean Jacques Rousseau. A fine companion book is that notable modern one, *How We Think*. However, since both of these are heavy, not easily digested books, those desiring a simpler work will make no mistake in choosing any one of the following: *Child Nature and Child Nurture,* St. John; *A Study of Child Nature,* Elizabeth Harrison; *A First Book in Psychology,* M. W. Calkins.

A knowledge of Bible history, manners and customs of the Bible times a prerequisite of the Sunday-school story-teller.—Lastly, whoever tells Bible stories should have a broad knowledge of Bible lands and times. He should know the customs of those who were the contemporaries of Abraham, Isaac, and Jacob, and something of the modes of life of Israel and her warrior kings. The following list comprises books that are delightful in their vivid splashes of the color of Palestine and full of inspiration. *Bible Manners and Customs,* G. M. Mackie; *A History of Old Testament Times in Palestine,* Shailer Mathews; *A History of Literature of Ancient Israel,* Henry Thatcher Fowler; *A Historical Geography of Bible Lands,* John B. Calkin.

This recommended course of preparation may seem a formidable task, and perhaps the question will arise as to whether or not it is all worth while. But there is no road to great achievement along any line except great labor, and the story-teller, as much as the painter, the sculptor, the author, and the musician, should be willing to toil and sacrifice, because he too is a maker of pictures and melodies, a creator of moods and ideals. If conditions make it impossible to cover as comprehensive a course as the one outlined, choose one book from under each heading and make a thorough study of that one. And if sometimes the process of preparation seems a grind for which there is not adequate reward, perhaps the worker will find courage in the magnificent creed of Richard Wagner: "And I believe that true disciples of pure art will be glorified in a divine atmosphere of sun-illumined, fragrant concords and united eternally with the Divine Source of all harmony."

Thought Questions

1. Of what value to the Sunday-school story-teller is an analytic study of great stories in the general field of literature?

2. Why is a study of fairy tales particularly helpful?

3. Of what value is an understanding of the principles of æsthetics?

4. Why should pictures and music supplement the story-telling work with children?

5. How does a knowledge of primitive religious beliefs aid the teacher in the Beginners and Primary Departments?

6. In what way does a knowledge of nature and the natural sciences aid the story-teller.

7. Why does the story-teller need to have some understanding of psychology?

8. Give reasons why it is necessary for the teller of Bible stories to know something of Bible history; of the customs of Bible times; of the geography of the Holy Land?

Assignment

Read the story of David playing before Saul, 1 Samuel 16. 14-23.

Write the story in your own words after this reading. Compare your version with that which follows.

Follow this by reading 1 Samuel 16. Study the map of Palestine for the location of Bethlehem; look up in the encyclopædia the customs of the Hebrew shepherds; read also chapters eleven and twelve of the first book of Ben Hur.

Write a second version of the story after this broader preparation and compare it with your first.

How David Used His Harp

Among the sunny hills of Bethlehem David, the shepherd boy, tended his sheep. He was a good shepherd, leading the flocks to green pastures and still waters, and watching all the while that no harm came to them. Sometimes he sang songs as he followed them over the slopes, and sometimes as he sang he played on a harp and made music that sounded far over the hills.

Now, it happened that in the same country there lived a king whose name was Saul. King Saul was very unhappy. He had been sick a long, long time, and nothing the doctors and wise men of the land could do had made him feel any better. He had forgotten how to smile, and because he had sad, gloomy thoughts all the while deep wrinkles came into his face.

One day some wise men began to wonder if music might make him happy and well again. They told their thoughts to the king, and he said, "Find a man who can play on the harp and bring him to me."

"There is a shepherd of Bethlehem who is skillful in playing," one of them said. "He is strong and kind and very fair to look upon. He is the son of Jesse and is called David."

A messenger was sent to seek him, and as David wandered here and there with the white flocks, petting the gentle ewes and watching that the lambs did not stray into dangerous places, word came that he should go to the king. His father gave him a present of bread and other good things to lay before King Saul. And then he set out upon his way.

When he came into the presence of the king he began to play. He played a song that he made for the sheep at evening when shadows were darkening the hills and he took them to the fold. Then he played a tune that the crickets and the quails and the wild rabbits stopped to hear, and the songs the people sang as they cut the grain and made merry at weddings. And the music pleased King Saul so much that he began to smile. He forgot the sad thoughts and felt better, and very soon he was well again. He was a very happy king now. And David was happy too. He was glad to think he had helped with his songs and his harp.

After that, whenever Saul was sick or in trouble, David played and sang for him and made him glad. And by and by he himself became king of Israel, and wrote for us many beautiful Psalms.

CHAPTER III

THE STORY-TELLER'S SPECIFIC PREPARATION

First step in specific preparation is a survey of the field.—Specific preparation to a story-teller is what making ready for a concert is to a musician. His foundation has been laid by mastery of the fundamentals of his art, his background enriched by broad knowledge of all pertaining to it. Now he applies principles and knowledge toward an artistic rendition of his program, in the hope of leaving an impression with his auditors that will not soon be effaced. And according to the greatness of soul of the performer, so will the result be. Like the man who has qualified in the science of engineering and goes out to solve through knowledge of that science some definite problem that will result in the creation of a bridge, tunnel, or breakwater that shall be a high light in the history of transportation, so the story-teller must solve his specific problem of awakening impulses and establishing ideals. And he must do this in exactly the way in which the engineer goes about making his tube, railway, or aqueduct.

Reading the Story.—He must survey the field. This means obtaining a clear conception of the plot of the tale he is to tell, which is accomplished by reading as a story is read for entertainment. But this reading is only the beginning of the preparation, as the student will realize if he attempts to recount the narrative to himself after this reading. Unless he has had much training, or is gifted with an unusually retentive memory, he cannot give it consecutively and smoothly. Instead of advancing step by step with the correct sequence of incidents, he will omit some necessary points and be obliged to go back and insert them. Why? Because reading a selection for entertainment is not analytical reading.

It is of utmost importance that this fact be grasped by everyone who aspires to become a successful teller of stories to children, because much of the poor narrating in both church and secular school is due to the teacher's snatching up a book at the last minute, reading the selection once, and then attempting to give it. The pianist at a recital would not dream of interpreting to his audience a musical composition unless he had gone over it many times, but leaders of children do that with stories very often. And then some of them wonder if, after all, the value of story-telling has not been greatly exaggerated.

Whoever works in this haphazard manner does an injury to a great art, an art that cannot fail to make the world a better and more enjoyable place, for whenever by slovenly preparation a story-teller fails to reach his hearers, he brings disrepute to the narrator's art among those who do not know its possibilities. His own sense of the value of that art diminishes and he sins against childhood.

Before attempting to tell any story he should know

the plot of that story as he knows the multiplication table. And he cannot know it without analyzing, without dissecting and examining each incident or picture in its regular order. After going over the tale to obtain a general idea of it, he should read it again, noting each incident in the order of its occurrence. The trained narrator can do this mentally, but the inexperienced one will advance more rapidly if he indicates on paper the several incidents, and numbers them.

I have been telling stories for many years, yet I still make this written note of plot incidents, and would never think of attempting to prepare a program without it. It fixes the sequence more quickly and firmly than anything else will do, and gives the narrator confidence that he is not going to forget and fail.

Suppose the story is "Water Turned Into Wine," from the second chapter of the book of John. The plot outline would read as follows:

Marriage in Cana; Jesus and disciples called.

Wine wanted; none on hand.

His mother advises the servants; waterpots set out.

Waterpots filled, as he bade.

Water drawn out, as he bade; taken to the governor, who found it turned to wine.

In a more complicated story, like that of "The Deluge," Genesis 6, 7, 8, the plot outline would read somewhat like the following:

A race of mighty men; all but Noah grew wicked as they grew in strength.

God grieved by wickedness; determines to destroy; bids Noah build ark.

Building of the ark; Noah's family go into ark; animals also.

The Flood.

The abating of the storm; Noah sends forth raven and dove; dove returns.

Sends out second time; returns with olive leaf.

Noah removes covering of ark; goes forth with family and animals.

Builds altar unto the Lord.

A rough outline of this kind makes it easy to review the story if one forgets the order in which events occur, and is the most helpful device for the student of which I know.

Visualizing the story—seeing the pictures.—Once the steps of a story are fixed in mind the narrator must visualize it, must see every picture composing it as clearly as he sees the painting that hangs on the wall of his home. If the tale is "Epaminondes and his Auntie," he must have a definite mental picture of a little pickaninny, the cabin that houses the auntie, and the old darkey woman in the sunshine of the dooryard or in the kitchen among the pots and pans. Some definite type of Negress, house and child must come before the mind's eye of the story-teller if he is to make the children see the characters. Each one must be glimpsed in its proper setting by the narrator or it will not be seen by his hearers. This does not mean that he should describe the house, the boy, or woman, and weary the auditors with unnecessary details; but unless he has seen them vividly before attempting to introduce them his rendition will fail to move either children or adults, because it will not ring with that reality that brings conviction and touches the emotional centers. The child nature is a delicately strung harp, and the untrained, unskillful hand that touches it awakens discords instead of harmonies. If this thought is borne in mind, slovenly and ineffective story-telling, of which we have so much to-day, will soon be a thing of the past.

Ability to visualize can be cultivated.—Ability to visualize a story does not require talent that is born with only a chosen few. Naturally, those possessed of vivid imaginations will find it easier than their colleagues who are not highly fanciful. But training and practice will bring a power of visualization that seems impossible to those who have not tried it; and this training does not necessitate isolation for study or going through any arduous grind. It may be had on the street, in the public amusement place, or in the homes of friends, for its foundation is close observation of every environment in which one happens to be placed, and afterward seeing that environment in memory as a little while before it was seen in reality. After passing a shop window try to visualize that window as it was when it met your eye. Name the articles in it and tell the relative position of each. Do this with your bedroom when you are out of it, with your library, the living rooms of your friends and the picture gallery where you sometimes go for entertainment. It will surprise you to know how carelessly you have observed until you attempt to give a description of familiar places. You will be equally surprised, after a little practice of this kind, to find how much more vividly you can see the pictures in a story than before. If the hero is a boy, what sort of looking boy is he? What is the color of his clothing, his hair, his eyes? If he goes to a village to get some groceries for his grandmother, is it a hamlet of thatched roofed cottages surrounded by cushions of turf, or a place of board shacks and bare dooryards—a mining town?

"In the country where a shepherd boy named David grew wise and good and became a king there is a town called Bethlehem.

"The houses of Bethlehem have been built on the side of a hill where the sun shines almost every day. They are made of stone. Around some of them are gardens where lilies and other flowers grow."

Stop and picture that country. Is it a land of high mountains and deep ravines, or of gentle hillslopes and sunny pastures? Are the streets narrow and winding, or do the houses clamber up the hillside in straight lines? Are there a dozen or more of these streets or only one or two? Historically and geographically your mental picture of Bethlehem may be far from correct, if your reading about the towns of Palestine has not been broad and detailed. But some definite picture of Bethlehem *must* be in your own mind or you cannot make it real to the child. You must see each object, each person and place mentioned, and if drill of this kind is persisted in for a little while, you will see each character and setting in every story you read. Remember that story-telling does not mean memorizing and repeating something that has been learned. It means making somebody else see and feel what you have seen and felt. The narrator is a creative artist, not a dramatic reader, and his mission is to paint with words as Landseer or Turner or Reynolds painted with pigments. There are pieces of literature that lose so much of their charm and effectiveness through reproduction that they should be read as the author wrote them. Good illustrations of such stories are Barrie's "Peter Pan," Maeterlinck's "Blue Bird," and René Bazin's "The Willow Taper." And in using the Bible stories, especially with older children, it is advisable to tell a portion of the tale and read another portion, that they may sense the beauty of expression that makes these tales without parallel in literature. For instance, in giving the account of the death of Lazarus, from the second chapter of the book of John, the narrator might tell in his own words the story of the sick man, of the sisters sending for Jesus, of the disciples pleading with him not to go back to Judæa, of his calming their fears, and of the succession of incidents that make up the tale until Martha meets Jesus and his comforting words to her. Then, in the beautiful language of the New Testament, let him continue thus: "Jesus said unto her, I am the resurrection and the life: he that believeth in me, though he were dead, yet shall he live. And whosoever believeth in me shall never die. Believest thou this?"

From this point the tale may be carried on to its conclusion, using the exact Bible wording in every instance where because of supreme beauty of expression, of some great message a phrase or sentence carries, or because it has become classic in history, it should be repeated and reiterated until stamped indelibly upon the mind of the child. Moreover, in telling Bible stories, when speaking of something that has been said by either Christ or God, artistry demands that the exact words be quoted. In such passages there should be no adaptation. Do not say, Jesus told her that her brother would rise again. Say "Jesus said unto her, 'Thy brother shall rise again.' " In long passages, as, for instance, where Noah is commanded to build the ark, in the sixth chapter of Genesis, it is permissible to say that the Lord told Noah to make a boat and to gather into it two of every sort of living thing, describing the boat and enumerating the animals according to the age and knowledge of the children. But there should be no adaptation of the short, exquisite passages that carry great lessons. Give such sentences as the Bible gives them. If there is a possibility that their full meaning may not be understood by the child, follow with some explanation. But in the actual telling of a story any other course of procedure would be inartistic, even if it were not irreverent.

However, unless, as stated above, exact dialogue is to be used, the language of the story should not be memorized. When the narrator actually knows and sees a story the telling becomes easy. The blacksmith who has no oratorical gifts can describe a horseshoe with facility because he knows horseshoes, and at mention of the word an image of an elliptical bar of steel comes before his eyes. A dentist can give a fascinating dissertation on the structure of teeth because he knows teeth, and the man who has lived in the woods can recount tales of birds and squirrels with such magnetism that he will draw a crowd. The old adage that knowledge is power has special significance for the story-teller, for out of knowing and seeing his tale comes power to tell it.

Getting the background and atmosphere of the story.—Another step in the story-teller's specific preparation is to obtain all the information possible about matters pertaining to the particular story he is to tell. If it is a tale of Japanese children, he should read something about child life in Japan, or of the coral carvers of Sicily if he is to give an anecdote of a Palermo boy and a coral medallion. Sara Cone Bryant has told in an exquisite and convincing manner the story of David and Goliath because she knows the Bible story in every one of its details, and because she knows enough of the life and ways in ancient Palestine to enable her to invest each situation with color and atmosphere. The student of story-telling needs to realize this. The more one knows of the environment in which the characters live, the keener becomes the visualization that is so necessary, and the more profoundly will the tale stir the child. Naturally, the amount of preparation will depend upon the time the worker has at his disposal and on the opportunity for research in his environment. But he should get something of the atmosphere of every story before he attempts to give it, or the telling will be of little avail.

This makes it clear why the teller of Old-Testament stories needs to study the customs of Old-Testament times. He needs to know something about the feasts of the Hebrews, the particular significance of the various books of the Bible, the religious sects of the Jews, their laws, customs, occupations and modes of dress. Without this knowledge he cannot touch the stories with the atmosphere they must have if they are to become as personal observances or experiences to the children. Moreover, to become familiar with the customs and ways of life of people of different times and lands is a part of the literary heritage of every child, and he cannot come completely into this heritage unless his teacher or guide already has that knowledge.

Securing dramatic suspense.—In the study of each story prepared for telling it is necessary to note the conflict that enters into it; to determine what opposing forces or characters make the dramatic suspense without which no tale can be of gripping interest. From the simplest fable to the most complicated story there is a strong element of suspense due to conflict. Take as an example the story of the building of the tower of Babel and the confusion of tongues, in the eleventh chapter of Genesis. The conflict lies between the determination of the people for self-glorification and the will of God. In the first chapter of the book of Job the element of conflict is in the effort of Satan to disprove Job's faith in God, and the man's struggle to bear his sufferings. This conflict and the suspense it engenders arouses children to a point of tense eagerness as to the result. Often this eagerness can be heightened by a pause and a deftly interpolated sentence, thus: "And God came down and saw the city and the tower. It grieved him to see how proud and boastful they were, and what *do* you think he did? He sent them away from the beautiful plain, and scattered them far and wide over the hills and valleys. And what was even harder for them, he gave each one—*a different language*. Then they could not understand each other. Men who had been friends could not tell one another the things that were in their hearts, but whenever they met they had to pass by like strangers. It was very, very sad for them."

There can be no story without this element of conflict. In everyone there is some difficulty, some predicament of character or characters. Determine what it is. Then make it clear to the child that there is a struggle, and set him aquiver with interest as to how it will end.

Practicing the story.—Practice the story. Tell it to yourself, to the tables and chairs, to an imaginary audience, aiming to make the rendition not only smooth and unhalting, but so dramatic that it cannot fail to catch and hold those who hear. The furniture and the family cat make an audience far preferable to the members of one's family or friends, because the thought of their criticism at seeing you do the unusual tends to stimulate self-consciousness and kill abandon. Tell it as when a child you told your mother about what happened at school, but smoothly and more artistically because of more knowledge. If you are filled with the spirit and atmosphere of the tale so that it becomes your own, this narration will be just as easy and joyous as was that of long ago. Remember that long association with characters is what makes possible artistic performance. If the general preparation has been broad and thorough, and you have lived the tale until you can abandon yourself to the telling without any thought of the mechanics of the process, the rendition will be spontaneous and natural. This is possible only when the story-teller is making no effort to remember somebody else's language, when he has no memory of printed page to bother him, when his eyes as well as his lips are giving the message.

Thought Questions

1. What do you understand by "specific preparation"?

2. Give the first step in the story-teller's specific preparation.

3. What is the value of outlining the plot of a story?

4. How may ability to visualize a story be developed?

5. Write a description of Bethlehem according to your visualization of it. (See paragraphs two and three, page 56.)

6. What is the value of visualizing a story?

7. What is meant by dramatic suspense in a story? How is such suspense secured?

8. Why is it necessary to practice telling a story before giving it to an audience? Is memorizing the aim of practice?

Class Assignment

Prepare for telling "Elisha Helping a Poor Widow," as given in 2 Kings 4. 1-7. After reading and analyzing the story, outlining the plot, and visualizing the scenes, write a description of Elisha, of the widow, and of her house and her two sons, according to your visualization of them.

Prepare for telling to a class of young children—Beginners or Primary—the story of "The Message of the Angel to Mary," Luke 1. 26-38, 46-56.

In making the preparation, keep in mind the successive steps as indicated in the above chapter.

CHAPTER IV

THE STORY-TELLER'S ATTITUDE

Appreciation of material.—Upon the narrator's attitude toward each individual story she is to tell will depend in large measure her success or failure. The worker, especially with little children, can have no better maxim to guide her in her efforts than these two: "Take your story seriously," and "If you cannot respect the story do not tell it." A tale that seems trivial to the teller cannot be given in a convincing, appealing manner, for the child will immediately sense a lack of sincerity. In a vague, indefinite way he realizes that it does not come from the heart. His interest and sympathy are not aroused and it is certain to fall upon stony ground. Moreover, the half apologetic rendition of one narrative will prejudice the hearer against the narrator in the future, for whoever has bored him once with artificiality that leaves him unthrilled and unswayed is listed in his mind as a poor story-teller, or as one whose collection of yarns is of inferior quality, and only by ingenious effort and much artistry can she gain his interest another time.

Every one with a first-hand knowledge of stories and childhood knows the truth of this statement out of his own experience. The professional in the public field and the mother in the home have each found out that if she does not like a tale, her child audience will not like it. And herein lies one of the most difficult problems the narrator has to solve, for with native temperament, environmental and hereditary influences each contributing its part toward shaping the individual taste, a type of story that is delightful to one may be obnoxious to another. Yet the hearing of each must be a period replete with joy to the child if the lesson it carries is to leave an indelible touch upon his nature. Therefore how is it possible, when material is not appealing to the teller, to give it with as much enthusiasm and sincerity as characterizes the narration of some favorite piece of literature?

Appreciation of aim.—The answer is by what Dr. Partridge calls "the persuasion of art." And artistic expression that quickens the feelings is redolent of truth, truth that rings with a clarion voice from the lips of one who has felt and believes in the message he is giving. Corot's "Man With the Hoe" brought about legislation in France to better the conditions of peasants there because the artist who painted it had seen and felt the plight of the man bowed down by his burden. By a year of study of peasant types in the fields beyond Paris, by actually living among the country folk and learning the limitations of their lives they awakened his interest and compassion. And the beholder senses to such a degree the truth and sincerity emanating from that canvas that it calls all latent sympathy into activity. It speaks as convincingly and unforgettably as a folk tale, and even if one desires to brush the theme from memory he can no more do it than he can forget the contour of an oak leaf or the smell of hay. To the artist who painted the picture that clumsy laborer spelled human soul and heart throbs, and he portrayed him with infinite care because of reverence for that heart and soul. Therefore the beholder feels that here is truth, here is reality. And truth, whether it speaks through marble, pen, or pigments, is the force that rocks the ages.

The story carries a message.—Truth speaks through the medium of the story as powerfully as from the canvass of the French painter, provided the tale is one that has stood the test and has survived with the good and great things that one generation passes on to another. Therefore every story worth the telling deserves the respect of whoever gives it because it carries a message to the child. It is an accumulation of the wisdom of the race, and any one to whom is granted the inestimable privilege of passing that wisdom on to childhood should realize that to him has been given a sacred trust as well as a glorious opportunity. Whether it be an extravaganza from the budget of some European grandmother, fairy narrative of beautiful imagery, or highly dramatic epic from the Book of Israel, somewhere among the meanderings of its plot is hidden a lesson for the listener, a lesson learned in life's school, and it is the business of the story-teller to study the tale until he finds that lesson, until he can determine wherein the dignity and value of that particular selection lies. Half the problem of the unappealing narrative is solved if this fact is remembered, if the story-teller will regard each contribution to the great literature of childhood as a sermon, and a far more effective sermon than one that is preached directly.

It is this quality of carrying a message, of touching some elemental, universal problem, that has made possible the longevity of the old, old tale, for nowhere does the law of the survival of the fittest hold more unvaryingly than in the field of literature. The meaningless and artificial yarn, the one that formalizes in the brain of him whose purpose is to win popular approval or wealth for himself is cast aside with the rubbish of the time in which it came into being. But the message-bringer and lesson-bearer, the one that has grown out of racial experience, out of deep conviction and sometimes out of heartbreak, whether it be folk tale, a novel of Hugo or Balzac, or a cross section of life from the pen of Tolstoy, survives that age and quickens souls in other ages because it is based upon some problem that touches human grief or happiness, and therefore helps to feed human desire.

Once the narrator comes into an appreciation of the aim and value of a tale, there will be no difficulty about giving it with enthusiasm and conviction. In the International Graded Courses the stories prepared by Miss Danielson and Miss Thomas are outlined and analyzed with such detail that the teacher cannot fail to see and appreciate the aim of each. But the Sunday-school worker needs to know how to take other material and fit it to his needs. Therefore it is just as necessary that he make an analytic study of stories

for the value of their content as for the structural
principles upon which they are built. A good plan
for the teacher of beginners' and primary classes is to
read the stories given in the leaflets or text books
before reading the note on preparation, or any of the
advisory material. Then set down on paper what
seems to be the purpose and aim of that story, and
compare your own deductions with the purpose of the
story as revealed in the circle talk, the lesson plans,
and preparatory note, and see how nearly you have
grasped the thought and aim behind the narrative.
After a little practice it will not be necessary to make
the written report, but it will still be the part of wisdom to read the tale *first,* and then think deeply regarding it before consulting the preparatory notes.
In no other way is ability to determine content values
acquired so quickly.

When the story is appreciated by the teller, when
she understands its meaning and message, she should
concentrate every effort toward getting that message
home to the child. And she can get it home to him
only by appreciating *him* and *his attitude,* as well as
the material she gives him.

Appreciation of the child and his attitude.—This
phase of appreciation is of paramount importance, for
the child heart and soul is the field in which the sower
plants the seed, and the husbandman who knows not
the quality of the soil of his farm plot reaps a scanty
harvest. In the early, formative period, when the
human sowing can be accomplished with such
exuberant blossoming at some future day, the child

in the Beginners and Primary Departments is athrill with eagerness to know. He is like a flower stretching its petals to the light, groping for food that his inner nature requires, and it is the mission of the story-teller to satisfy this appetite with wholesome and abundant nourishment. The story brings to him the knowledge he is seeking, and therefore it is the most serious thing in the world to him. He believes in it as he believes in his mother, and to discover that the narrator does not believe is a shock to his vibrant, yearning nature. The world is so big and he is so little and helpless, and often he feels a sense of bewilderment and loneliness. Adults who have not lived close to the heart of childhood do not always realize this, but it is a poignant truth, one that some of us know out of memories of our own early years. It is of vital importance that the narrator realize it, for the story brings to little people that sense of warmth and comfort that is craved in solitary hours. The knowledge that out of hard situations good issues come, the learning that one is rewarded just for being good and doing right, as always happens in the great tales of childhood, is his compensation for being little in a vast and bewildering world. He appreciates to the uttermost the events and characters in a story that feeds his desires, and this appreciation means far more to him than just entertainment. While he listens to that which he enjoys he is unconsciously choosing and evaluating. He is casting out in his own mind that which is undesirable, is keeping that which is to be desired, and is establishing standards. And in

the great tales that have survived the ages, the match-
less narratives in which truth sounds through a trum-
pet, the good looms with beauty and power and the
bad is repellent and ugly. Appreciation on the part of
the child causes him to realize this to a very high degree. But this appreciation must begin in an earlier
time with appreciation of both story and child by the
story-teller. And this appreciation secured, great and
lasting results are certain to crown the work of the
narrator, for then he will be able to give his material
with the persuasion of art, which is but another way of
saying that he will portray truth convincingly.

Truth portrayed convincingly is the mightiest force
the world has ever known. There are many examples
to substantiate this statement. The glorification of
dying for one's fatherland by the poets of four thousand years has led men to rush eagerly toward suffering and death upon the battlefield. The fact that vice
is surely punished and virtue is rewarded, powerfully
portrayed by the narrative and pictorial art of every
land, has established a belief in the inexorable workings of the law of compensation even before, out of
first-hand experience, one has learned the truth of that
law. Art broadens the world and enlarges the vision.
It expands the narrow dooryard into the universe,
because art is built upon truth. And art can make the
child what we want him to be, provided whoever
guides him can make truth convincing to him. Because the great creators in every field know this so
well we find a Claude Lorrain studying the sunsets on
the Campagna while the pleasure-loving Romans were

merrymaking along the vias; Hugo and Balzac forsaking comfortable quarters for the misery of the Paris Montmartre; a Coquelin sojourning in a madhouse that he might act the part of a maniac so convincingly as to sway his audiences. And because the story reflects life, to every child taking his first steps upon the path his elders have already trod, art, the narrator's art, will do for him what down the long flight of the ages it has done for the world: it will teach him lessons he needs to learn, lessons that will arouse in him an appreciation of humility, beauty, truth, tenderness, and reverence, provided the teacher who guides his thought processes understands the dignity and value of every tale she tells, and realizes that in the great literature of childhood there are no meaningless or artificial tales, any more than in the realm of nature there is an unnecessary or ugly leaf.

Thought Questions

1. Why is it necessary for the story-teller to take the tale seriously?
2. What do you understand by respecting a story?
3. How can a sense of appreciation of the aim and value of a story be developed?
4. In general, what is the attitude of the child toward the story?
5. Of what value to the child is his appreciation of a story?
6. Explain how, through the story, the child learns that it is sometimes desirable to experience hard situations.
7. What is meant by "the persuasion of art"?

8. What is the value of portraying truth convincingly?

ASSIGNMENT

What is the definite message to the child in each of the following stories:

Crossing the Red Sea, Exodus 14.
The Triumphant Song of Israel, Exodus 15.
The Five Thousand Miraculously Fed, John 6. 1-13.
The Story of Jonah, Jonah 1. 3.
Ezra's Explanation of the Law, Nehemiah 8. 1-12.

CHAPTER V

HOW TO TELL THE STORY

The story-teller must have confidence.—When the narrator faces her audience of little people she must do it with confidence in herself that she is going to interest and hold them. Broad knowledge concerning the tale, its characteristics, theme, and aim will cause the plot to unroll spontaneously and smoothly. Living with it during the course of preparation until it becomes part of the experience will put self-consciousness to wing, and, as Georg Ebers used to say of his Egyptian tales, "The story tells itself." And the thing that concerns the teller is that it shall tell itself in the best possible manner.

The manner of the story-teller.—*Be natural.* This is the first requisite of good story-telling, and earnest study will secure naturalness just as surely as a systematic saving of pennies will put dollars into the bank account later on. Of the method of preparation enough has been said already. The point to remember now is this: Describe the pictures that come before your eyes in *your* way, not in imitation of somebody else's rendition. Be yourself, yourself at your very best, and in order to be this it is necessary to take stock of your assets and liabilities before you face your audience. If you slouch as you sit or stand, learn how to poise and keep your body under control. Tone down your voice and modulate it if it is sharp, monotonous, or in any way unpleasing. Remember that nothing is impossible to him who keeps his eye single and his purpose fixed, and that a stutterer in old Athens became the mightiest orator of Greece. I have seen awkward girls reconstruct themselves into beautifully poised women, girls who in the beginning were so crude that their ambition to become story-tellers was a source of mingled amusement and pity to their friends. Yet they succeeded in accomplishing the seemingly impossible because they set out with determination and never deviated from their purpose. Anyone possessed of intelligence and will power can do as much.

The voice of the story-teller.—In speaking of voice improvement a word of caution is necessary. To make the voice pleasing does not mean to use a sugary tone, or, as Sara Cone Bryant says, "A super-sweetened whine," which always brings failure because the child detects affectation behind it. It means smoothing off the rough edges, as carpenters say, removing throaty or nasal defects, if you have them. It means polishing your tones so they do not jar upon the ear of the hearer, yet keeping them still your natural, speaking ones. It means securing purity, clearness, and distinct enunciation without making any tone or modulation seem exaggerated.

The question of gesture.—In order to bring vividness to the child it is not necessary to turn into a gymnast or gesticulator. The work of the story-teller is precisely opposite to that of the actor, and while the artist of the stage must represent what happens in a drama, the business of the narrator is to describe. By his words he must picture the scenes before his mental vision so graphically that his hearers see them as clearly as he does, and therefore he must not attract attention to himself. Instead, he must lead the audience away from himself into the midst of the scenes he describes. He must not obtrude his personality upon them in such a way that they are conscious of it and divide their attention between the teller and the tale. Consequently everything not necessary to portraying the scenes must be kept in the background. This applies especially to the question of gesture, in which the beginner is always interested, and which often proves to be the rock upon which he meets disaster. Gesture should be a part of story-telling only when it forces itself in, when it is one of the narrator's natural forms of expression. If you gesticulate as you talk you will not be able to keep gesture out of your story-telling, and in that case it will improve the rendition because it helps to secure naturalness. But if it is studied and artificial, it will destroy the unity of scenes and divert attention from story to performer. So, because your colleague uses a shoulder shrug or an arm movement with fine effect it does not follow that you should use it. If you appreciate your tale and the message it carries, you will be so full of it that in your eagerness to get it home to your hearers you will not stop to think whether you should wave a hand or point a foot at a certain word or phrase. Gesture will take care of itself, just as it does when you re-count the escape of the small boy you saw pulled from in front of an automobile, or of the woman who was rescued from the blazing house, and the narration will ring with the conviction that always characterizes whatever comes from the heart. On the other hand, if the thought of the teller is on gesture rather than on the scenes of the story, he will fall into many errors and his efforts cannot possibly bring gratifying results.

This is why it so often happens that out of the preaching of street exhorters of little or no education have come movements that have swayed cities and nations. The speaker believed in the message he was giving, and in his eagerness to make others see as he saw, everything else was swept from his mind. The street cars and the passing throng did not disturb him, and men who stopped out of curiosity soon caught the earnestness of his appeal and it began to sway them. This has happened so often and in so many localities, especially during strikes, that it has come under the observation of almost everyone. And always the se-cret of the success of these men in obtaining followers has been belief in the message they were giving and knowledge of the conditions against which they were crying. Did they study effects? No! When the heart is full to overflowing we do not have time to think of devices for making ourselves appealing, and we do not need to, for the overflow from one pulsing heart waters the dry places in other hearts.

Taking one's time.—Story-telling should be a leis-urely process. To hurry means to blur the pictures

that come before the mental vision of the child, and
unless each scene that contributes to the plot is vivid
and realistic the tale fails in its purpose. The narrator
must feel that the floor is his, and that he has time
enough for the portrayal of every shade of meaning
he wishes to convey. There are portions of a story
in which accelerated speech heightens the effect, while
to move deliberately would be to mar it. But this does
not mean hurrying in the sense of rushing to get
through. If the narrative you have begun is too long
to fit into the time at your disposal, do not attempt to
complete it before the bell rings or signal sounds and
spoil it for the child. Make it a continued tale, but
make the section given a complete chapter, and say,
"Next week I'll tell you how the lost boy found his
mother." The interest of the children will not lag
because the selection is broken into parts, but it will
have only half the effect it should have if they feel
that you are hurrying to get through. They will begin to think of the time of dismissal or of change of
classes, and interest will be on the wane. But it is imperative, in case your memory is poor, that you make
a note of just where you stopped, so that there shall
be no uncertainty on your part as to where to begin
again, and the children discover you are not as much
interested in the story as they are.

Covering mistakes.—The well-prepared narrative
is seldom forgotten in the telling, but if some necessary detail slips from your mind, contrive to bridge
over the gap in such a way that your hearers do not
realize your predicament. The story is so real and

serious to the child that for him to learn that his
mother or teacher does not know what happens next
mars his joy in it and shakes his faith in the teller.
Manufacture another detail or pass on to the next step
and connect it with what has gone before so that he
has no suspicion you have suffered a lapse of memory.
The story-teller, like the actor, must learn to cover up
his mistakes and to keep his head upon all occasions.

Suppose the selection to be related is that of the
gathering of funds for repairing the Temple, 2 Kings
12, and you forget to mention at the proper place the
detail of Jehoiada boring a hole in the lid of the chest
and setting it beside the altar. Since this is a necessary link in the chain of the story, it must be inserted.
And it can be done without spoiling the narrative for
the child, and without his discovering that you have
forgotten. Miss Thomas retells it in the primary
stories of the International Graded Courses something
after this fashion: "The priests kept the money that
was given. They asked their friends for more. One
would think there might have been money enough, but
there was not. Still more was needed."

(At this point the detail of the preparation of the
chest should be inserted.)

Suppose the story-teller forgets to do this and dis-
covers a little later that a necessary detail has been
omitted. He can bridge over the gap thus: "So the
king asked the people to come to the Temple and bring
an offering. The people were glad to help and did
as he bade them. They came from all over the country. They gave money to the priests. The priests put

the money into a chest that stood at the side of the altar. It was a big chest; and very strong and heavy. In the top was a hole big enough for all the gold and silver pieces to slip through. Jehoiada, the priest, had cut the hole there and made the chest ready as soon as the king told the priests they would mend the Temple."

Changes of voice in telling a story.—Make the tone of voice fit the characters. Remember that giants are not silvery-tongued like beautiful princesses, and that the gentle grandmother speaks in a softer key than the one used by the wicked witch. Keep the voice true to the various roles if you wish to bring vividness to the child. It is a good plan to practice the colloquy of the witches, giants, fairies, and other personages that move through the tale until the change from one voice to another is easy and spontaneous. One may have a clear idea as to how the tones should sound, but only by hearing ourselves give them can we know whether they ring with realism or affectation. And as they seem to us, so will they seem to the children. Sometimes in speaking the part of a giant, or of a squeaky-voiced old woman, if it is an unaccustomed role, self-consciousness and diffidence make the tones seem artificial even when they typify excellently the personages in mind. Practice will remedy this, and after a few repetitions we can give them with abandon. And by practice, by doing many times the same bit of dialogue, one learns which of several pitches is best. And having learned the best, the story-teller can make it his own. Professional narrators are doing this constantly, and the beginner will make a grave mistake if he attempts to get along without it. Joseph Jefferson was a king of the stage, yet he said he never had sufficient time for the preparation of any role he played. Even after he was famous as the portrayer of Rip Van Winkle he practiced one of Rip's calls to his dog in seventeen different ways to see if he could find a more effective method of giving it.

In all the Bible stories in which there is much dialogue the story-teller should endeavor to make the voice fit the characters as he visions them. Try to portray the voices of Samuel and Saul in the story of Saul's dethronement foretold, 1 Samuel 15. Other Bible stories in which change of voice in the dialogue will make the telling more effective are: The Five Thousand Fed, John 6. 1-13; The Meal and Oil that Did Not Fail, 1 Kings 17. 8-16; The Blind Man Cured, John 9. 1-11.

Vary the tone in narrative portions as much as in the dialogue. To suddenly drop the voice low after one has been speaking in the usual conversational tone tends to heighten the suspense. This is especially helpful when children begin to show inattention. Quiet begets quiet, whereas noise and restlessness summon their own kind. Another aid in securing interest when it shows signs of wandering is to speak the name of a child thus: "And, John, then the thunder came"; or, "You three boys in the back row never can guess what happened next." The personal equation enters. The inattentive child begins to feel that the story is being told especially for him and he listens again.

The pause in telling a story.—Nothing is more effective in heightening dramatic effect of a tale, especially near the climax, than the sudden, unexpected pause, the pause in the middle of the sentence or just after the opening words. "And then—two big eyes shone through the darkness;" or, "The boy ran without stopping until he came to the injured dog, and the big, shaggy fellow—looked up and wagged his tail." "The priests took up the ark and carried it to the edge of the river and stepped into the water. As they did this the river—stopped flowing in its regular way." "When he reached Jerusalem Jesus went to the Temple, but—he did not stay there long."

The use of pictures in telling a story.—The use of pictures in telling a story is of tremendous value, provided they are handled with smoothness and artistry. But I have seen what promised to be a splendid piece of story-telling end in failure because illustrative material was used in such a way that it diverted interest from the tale. There are several methods that bring gratifying results, and it is for the individual to decide which he can use to the best advantage. Some workers show illustrative material before telling the story and make it the object of discussion. Others make an observation of pictures and objects an aftermath to the tale, and some show them during the process of narration. Inasmuch as story-telling belongs to the field of art, the worker in its ranks should be privileged to manipulate his materials in the way he can use them most effectively. Therefore to tell him when or where to exhibit a picture is to hamper instead of aid him.

In my own programs I sometimes use one method and sometimes another, and sometimes a combination of the three. It is a matter for each worker to decide for himself, because success with object work depends upon the type of tale, upon the children, and upon the teller's mood. The inexperienced narrator usually finds it easier to precede or follow the story with pictures or objects, although I have known beginners who were remarkably skillful in introducing them during the course of the narration. The point to remember in doing this is that they must be brought in so as to seem part of the tale, never as outside material that breaks the plot thread. They should be at the teller's hand and arranged as the lecturer with a balopticon arranges his slides. Otherwise they will seem to the child irrelevant to the story, and by a scattering of interest he will lose part of the value of both picture and tale. Do not say, "Now I shall show you a picture of a shepherd boy like David," and then proceed to hold up the picture. Say instead, "He was a gentle-faced lad with soft hair and shaggy skin clothes, and he carried a crook, just like the boy in this picture. And the sheep were white and fleecy, like this mother and her two lambs."

The same method should be employed in using drawings to illustrate a story. Do not stop unwinding the thread of the narrative and have the class wait while you make a sketch on the blackboard. Draw the tale, or let the chalk do it as you tell it instead of halting the action while you illustrate. The teacher who can sketch in a sheepfold or hillside as she re-

counts the exploits of David, who can by a few curves
and lines show the relative position of the good boy
and the fierce giant, is fortunate indeed, for the crud-
est of drawings have a vivifying power to the child,
provided they are made to fit into the story and are
done while his imagination is working to full capacity,
so that he mentally completes the picture that is outlined before his eyes. It requires some talent to sketch
men, women, pigs, and cows into a tale, but a few
strokes will indicate a tree or peasant house or king's
castle, or a seashore with boats sailing into the blue
unknown. And to little children those few strokes
made during the telling of the tale mean more than a
finished production after the narrative is completed.

As stated in a previous chapter, practice telling the
story to an imaginary audience as you would tell it
to a real one, using pictures, objects, drawings, and
whatever material you believe will facilitate your work.
Then face your class strengthened by preparation and
belief, and *be natural*. Let the thought of the fragrance of the flower gladden your sowing of the seed,
remembering that the story lived in childhood is quite
certain to become a blossoming tree of fragrance and
beauty in later years.

THOUGHT QUESTIONS

1. Why is it a mistake for the story-teller to imitate
the manner of another?

2. What points should be kept in mind in attempting to improve the manner of telling a story?

3. How may voice improvement be secured without affectation?

4. Why is it a mistake to practice specific gestures to use in telling a story?

5. In what way is it possible to avoid hurrying if a story is too long to tell during the time at one's disposal?

6. Why is it advisable to change the voice in dialogue portions of a story? In narrative portions?

7. How should pictures and objects be used in story-telling to secure the best results?

Assignment

Study the story of Queen Esther, Esther 3, 4, 5, 6, 7. Retell this story in your own words, bearing in mind the idea of changing the voice wherever such changes will serve to make the tale vivid.

CHAPTER VI

PRACTICE IN CONDENSATION

The story-teller versus the dramatic reader.—The popular idea of the story-teller as a sort of public reader or elocutionist who finds a tale in a book, memorizes and then recounts it to an audience is very far from being true. A rendition of this kind may be excellent as a dramatic reading, but it is *not* story-telling, never was considered story-telling by those who knew what constituted the narrator's art, and never will be. Yet so often even professional entertainers err in announcing that they will tell a story when they give a reading that it is important that the beginner shall understand the difference. And herein lies the difference: To give a reading means to memorize a selection and then recite it to an audience. To tell a story is to describe the pictures or incidents that make up the plot of the tale, as the teller sees them *at that time,* and in the words that occur to him *at that time.* Not long ago I heard a professional entertainer say she would tell the story of Epaminondes and his Auntie. But she did not tell the story of Epaminondes. She had memorized word for word the version of the tale that Sara Cone Bryant gives, and then recited it. As a reading the performance was creditable. As story-telling it was a pitiful failure, and by those who knew she was very disparagingly criticized for claiming to do some-

85

thing she did not do. To use a common expression, she was sailing under false colors, which is something the true artist will never stoop to do.

The rearrangement of material.—The specific preparation of the story-teller often means much more than analyzing a tale that is already in shape for telling, visualizing its scenes and incidents, and living with them until they become personal experiences. Not infrequently he must reconstruct or adapt his material, for many a narrative not in proper form for telling carries a message so important to the child that he cannot afford to leave it out of his programs. Sometimes a selection that in style and language is suited to adolescents, or even adults, can be simplified into a joy-bringer to little people. Sometimes one that is too long and rambling requires condensation. And very often it happens that an entire rearrangement of incidents is necessary, as, for instance, in a tale where the action moves backward from the climax to illustrate cause and effect. And sometimes an incident in a book of history, biography, or a magazine is so fraught with meaning to boys and girls that it deserves amplification into a story for telling. Of these several processes the narrator must be master. And this mastery places him in the same class with the creative artist, the author who writes a novel around the life of some man or woman whose story he has heard, or the composer who makes a folk song the nucleus of a suite or Hungarian Rhapsody.

The successive steps in condensation.—Of the several processes of adaptation, condensation, and elimination, condensation is one most easily handled by the beginner, and the one the average worker will have occasion to use most frequently. And condensation is so easy, once the underlying principles are understood, that by its use even the beginner can multiply his stock of tales.

Condensation begins with analyzing the story to get a clear idea of the plot. Then follows the cutting away of everything that can be omitted and yet keep a clear and connected narrative. Description may give a very beautiful touch to the written story, but it has no place in the oral one, where every minute something must be happening. Therefore all description should be eliminated, and the setting or locality in which the action transpires must be made clear by a phrase here, an explanatory clause there. This is exactly what is done in the folk tale, where a few skillful touches give a graphic picture of the scene through which the characters move. Thus we find in some of the great racial tales such bits as these: "In a lonely valley in China"; "Far up in the north country on a snow-covered mountain peak"; "In a forest bright as a rainbow with frost painted autumn leaves." All these are parts of sentences in which characters are introduced, yet they give to the child, who thinks concretely, as definite an idea of locality as a paragraph of description. Note these vivid touches in some Bible stories: "Naboth the Jezreelite had a vineyard, which was in Jezreel, hard by the palace of Ahab, king of Samaria"; "And he removed from thence to a mountain on the east of Bethel, and pitched his tent, having Bethel on the west and Hai on the east; and there he builded an altar unto the Lord." Not an unnecessary phrase is used in any of these, yet immediately one visions something of the character of the country in which their events transpire.

The beginner in the field of story-telling will find a study of captions or descriptive titles on the screens of moving-picture houses very helpful. In fact, many of the principles that apply to photoplay construction apply also to the work of the oral story-teller, who must secure vividness with brevity and completeness without nonessentials.

Elimination of minor or unnecessary incidents.— If in the chain of incidents that make the plot thread there are those of minor importance, they too should be cut away. By incidents of minor importance is meant those that are not actually necessary to the telling of the tale, even though in the written narrative they give emphasis and contribute considerably toward characterization. Every happening not necessary to make clear to the child why the story ends as it does should be cut away, for only by this means can there be the simplicity of plot and clear sequence which the oral narrative demands. There is a type of tale like Epaminondes of the plantation mammy, and "Stupid Hans" of Grimm, in which there is practically no plot, the entire aim of which is to accentuate stupidity or some other characteristic. The charm and value of such stories lies in the numerous incidents of the same kind. And this is often the case in short, simple narratives used to point a moral or specific truth. But where there is a plot sufficiently complicated to make it gripping, numerous incidents tend to confuse. Therefore, unless each dovetails naturally into the succeeding one and contributes something to it or to the final outcome of the story, it should be cut away, although in itself it may be a very charming or moving incident. As she cuts or prunes some classic for oral use, the story-teller should remember that by this process she is bringing the beautiful original within the enjoyment of the child. For the boy or girl who has been held fascinated by a plot will listen eagerly afterward to the reading of that story, or will read it for himself, thereby coming into appreciation of the beauty of style and expression of the master he might never acquire had he not been introduced to it previously through the medium of a condensed story.

In some stories several incidents, each of equal importance, not dependent upon each other but contributing toward the final outcome of the plot, are used to indicate some pertinent vice or virtue, such as weakness, generosity, gratitude, faithfulness, or untruthfulness; or to indicate failure or success. In this event, where one incident alone would make the characteristic apparent, and the series serves only to emphasize it, choose the one that is most appealing to you, and with that one bring the truth home to the child. This method is far preferable to that of using several incidents, for the employment of a series of independent events tends to deviate the hearer's attention from the main plot thread.

Elimination of characters.—Eliminate characters as well as incidents, the secondary, unimportant person-

ages that often heighten the local color and charm of
the written narrative, but that do not contribute anything toward its action and climax. The process of
elimination thus resolves itself into the cutting away of
description, of irrelevant or unnecessary events. and
unnecessary characters. As suggested before, the explanatory phrase or sentence as the characters are introduced indicates where the action transpires, and if
it shifts to a locality that affects the destinies of the
personages and has an influence upon the final outcome
of the plot, another bit of explanation or side remark
will be all that is required to bring a picture of the
new region to the mind of the child. As a great French
story-teller said not long ago: "Strip the tale bare to
its plot thread. Then reclothe it as Worth or Paquin
robes a lovely woman, using no garment for itself,
but because each fold of chiffon and strip of lace or
satin serves to accentuate the beauty and charm of
the wearer."

Unifying the story.—After elimination and condensation is complete the next step is unifying the
story. This is very important, for after much material has been cut away some artistry is necessary in
welding the remainder into form again, lest it be disconnected and jumbled instead of smooth and finished.
The beginner at adaptation work will do well to write
the revised version, for the written form reveals crudities the novice might overlook otherwise. The condensed tale should be as smooth and flowing as the
original, and a little practice will enable one to interpolate a phrase here and a word there so as to bridge

over the gap caused by the elimination of a page or paragraph. The story must not sound "as if it has holes in it," as a small boy once said about a tale he had heard given by a beginner at condensation work. After a few trials the writing will not be necessary, for practice will give facility and a sense of perspective that will enable one to connect and unify while working orally. But the beginner should not attempt to reshape material without writing it.

Rearranging a story.—More difficult than condensation, but just as necessary an equipment for the storyteller is rearranging a tale, to twist it so the middle or end of the written narrative becomes the beginning of the spoken one. Yet the mastery of a few principles makes it not beyond the accomplishment of any worker with children. For this, as for condensation, it is necessary to analyze the story to determine where the plot begins, and to roughly outline the action as it moves toward the climax, remembering that not every story opens with the beginning of the plot. Sometimes it begins with the middle and sometimes with the end and works back to the beginning. But the oral narrator must begin with the *logical* starting point, and usually with the leading character, because any other method brings less vivid pictures to the child.

If this thought is borne in mind, once the logical starting point is determined, rearrangement is no more difficult for the beginner than condensation.

One of the loveliest of all the Bible stories is that of Ruth. To the little child and to the gray-haired man it is equally appealing, and when the entire book of

Ruth is condensed and simplified so as to be within the understanding of very young boys and girls, its beauty and sweetness makes an impression upon them that they do not forget. Prepared to tell to primary children it would read something like this:

Ages and ages ago, in a land called Canaan, people were suffering because of a famine. A famine is a time of very little food, when there are no harvests to gather and everybody is hungry for days and weeks. Many different things may cause a famine. Sometimes crops dry up and die because very little rain falls. Sometimes a flood sweeps over a country and destroys them. And sometimes they are eaten by insects. The people of Canaan were starving and dying, for everybody suffers in a time of famine, even the rich. But the poor suffer most, because they never have enough money to buy food from those who have it. So they must either starve or go away.

Because they could see nothing else to do, some of the people of Canaan left their homes and went to the land of Moab, where there was food for all. Among these was a man named Elimelech, who had a wife and two sons, Mahlon and Chilion.

Soon after reaching Moab Elimelech died, and his wife Naomi was left alone with her boys. They must have felt very sad and forsaken in a country of strangers, but because they could get no food in their own land they could not go back. But the people were kind to them in their sorrow, and by and by they began to feel at home. The sons each married a woman of the Moabites. One of these was named Orpah and the other was called Ruth, and they and Naomi dwelt together and were happy.

Years passed, years of peace and pleasure for the family of Elimelech. Then Death knocked at the door. Mahlon and Chilion were taken, and again

Naomi was left alone, this time with the wives of her sons.

Then she thought longingly of Caanan, where her people dwelt. She wanted to go back and live among those of her own blood, and one day word came that made her know she could go. God had sent abundant crops to Canaan's hills and plains. The wheat and barley harvests were heavier than ever they had been before. The famine time was over and days of plenty had come.

Naomi loved her daughters-in-law very much, and they loved her. But she felt she ought not to ask them to leave their own country and kindred, for she knew they would be lonely and sad in a strange land, even as she had been when first she went to Moab. So she said to them: "Return each of you to your mother's house; and the Lord deal kindly with you, as ye have dealt with the dead, and with me."

By these words she meant that the two women had been so good to her dead sons and to her that God would surely reward them.

Ruth and Orpah wept at Naomi's words, for they loved her so much they could not bear to think of parting from her. Orpah kissed her good-by and started back to her own mother's house. But Ruth would not go. She clung to Naomi's hand and said, "Entreat me not to leave thee, or to return from following after thee; for whither thou goest, I will go, and where thou lodgest, I will lodge; thy people shall be my people, and thy God my God."

This was another way of saying: "Do not send me away. I want to go wherever you go and to live where you live. I want your people to be my people and your God shall be my God."

Do you think anybody could have sent Ruth away when she begged and wept so? Naomi did not send her. She let her go along, and after many days' travel they came to Bethlehem, the place that had been Naomi's home. It was very lovely then, for it was summer time, and just at the beginning of the barley harvest.

Because they had little money Ruth said to Naomi, "Let me go and glean in the grain fields to get food for both of us." "Go, my daughter," was Naomi's answer. So Ruth went to a field that belonged to a man named Boaz, who was a kinsman of Naomi, and so rich that he had much land and many men-servants and handmaidens. Men-servants and handmaidens are people who work for somebody else.

One day as Ruth was gleaning among the grain heads, Boaz came into the field and saw her.

"Whose damsel is this?" he said to the servant who was watching over the reapers.

The man told him she was a woman of the Moabites who had come back with Naomi.

Now, Boaz had heard the story of her devotion to Naomi, how she had left her father, mother, and the land of her birth to go with the lonely woman. As he looked into her sweet face and clear eyes he knew all the good that had been said of her was true. He wanted to reward her as she deserved to be rewarded, so he told some of his men-servants to pull barley stalks out of the bundles and scatter them in her way, that her work might not be so hard. Ruth was so thankful when she found Boaz was making it easy for her to find grain to glean that she seemed more sweet and good than ever. Day after day she toiled in the corn and barley fields until the end of the harvest. At meal time she sat with the other reapers and ate of the parched corn that was their food. And every night she went back to the house of Naomi.

Now, it happened that the field in which Ruth was gleaning had belonged to Naomi's husband, Elimelech, who lost it during the famine time. Naomi began to wonder how she might redeem it, or get it back for herself and Ruth, for it was a custom in those days, that if a man lost his home or anything that he owned, after he died some kinsman, brother, uncle, cousin, or even second cousin, must, if he could, buy it back for his wife and children. So she sent Ruth to Boaz to see if they might obtain this field, and to tell him that he was her kinsman, for in some way it happened that he did not know it. Perhaps his father was Naomi's father's great-uncle, and nobody had ever thought to tell him anything about it. Perhaps he was the son of her second or third cousin. We do not know how they were related, for they were of such very distant kin that Boaz himself did not know it. But because he was a good man he wanted to do what was right. He said to her, "Tell Naomi that there is a kinsman nearer than I. If he will not do the part of a kinsman, then will I do it." He meant that he would redeem the field for Naomi if the other man did not.

Early the next morning Boaz went to the gate of the city and sat down. Soon Naomi's other kinsman came by, and they talked about the field.

"If thou wilt redeem it, redeem it," Boaz said, "but if thou wilt not redeem it, then tell me that I may know, for there is none to redeem it beside thee, and I am after thee."

They went over everything that would have to be done. The barley field was worth a great deal of money, so the other man said he could not redeem it, because he was poor.

He drew off his shoe and handed it to Boaz.

"Redeem thou the field," he said.

Boaz took the shoe, and called out in a voice so loud that all who were passing might hear: "Ye are witnesses that I have this day redeemed the field that belonged to the husband of Naomi."

That was a way of saying that he promised the peo-

ple of the city to do what was right by his kinswoman.
The passing of a shoe from one to the other was a way
they had in those days of binding a promise.

Boaz kept his word. The field of her husband went
back to Naomi, and she was no longer a poor woman
who had to toil for her bread.

But that was not all. He made another promise that
day as he sat by the gate. He said he would take Ruth,
the Moabite, to be his wife, for he had been so pleased
by her beauty and sweet ways as he had watched her
in the fields that he wanted to have her with him
always.

So the woman who had left her country to keep another woman from being sad was married to the owner
of the fields. Never again did she need to glean among
the corn and barley stalks as one of the handmaidens,
but lived like a princess in the great house of a rich,
good man. Naomi dwelt with them in their beautiful
home, and years of contentment and happiness for all
three of them passed in the pleasant land of Canaan.

THOUGHT QUESTIONS

1. What is the difference between giving a reading
and telling a story?

2. What is the first step in condensing a story?

3. What material should be eliminated from a story
in condensing it?

4. What do you understand by unifying a story?

5. How would you proceed to rearrange a story?

ASSIGNMENT

Condense and prepare for telling to a group of
Primary children the story of Isaac and Rebekah,
Genesis 24. 1-67.

Condense and prepare for telling to a group of Beginners the story of Samuel, 1 Samuel, chapters 1-3.

CHAPTER VII

PRACTICE IN ELABORATION

Ability to amplify a qualification of the story-teller.—Sometimes it happens that an incident contains a lesson the child should learn, and is so dramatic that within it lie elements of a splendid story, but is too condensed in form, too meager in detail, and too explanatory in diction to be a tale for telling. In such a case amplification is necessary, and ability to amplify can be acquired by every story-teller, even though not to such a degree as to make him famous. The man or woman of mediocre talent will not become a de Maupassant or Daudet because he takes a course in short-story writing; nor can he hope to qualify as a narrator of the power of Scheherazade, no matter how much he studies the principles of construction and delivery. That elusive, undefinable thing which we call genius is the line of demarcation between those ordinarily endowed and those supremely gifted, and only the latter can mount the highest peaks of artistic success. But anyone can learn to amplify and build stories from bare anecdotes that will be enjoyed by a child.

This ability to amplify is especially necessary to those who will tell Bible stories to children, because in both the Old and the New Testament it often happens that two or three verses contain the nucleus of an ab-

sorbing story, provided implied details are supplied
and the situations invested with sufficient local color
to make them realistic. Take, for instance, Genesis
37. 1-3. Here is the framework of a very charming
story, that of the son who was so dear to his father
that he fashioned for him a coat of many colors. But
to tell to the little child the bare plot outline given in
these verses will make not much of an impression upon him. The picture needs to be vivified by supplying
everything that is implied. The worker in the Beginner's and Primary Departments must realize that
the little people under her tutelage are living in a narrow environment. Their knowledge is extremely limited because their experience has been limited. They
are interested chiefly in the home circle, in their pets,
and in the beings that have been part of their experience. Consequently, their imaginations do not range
far afield, and they cannot, in fancy, supply the background that makes the story real. The characters must
be brought to them and shown in conditions parallel to
those that they know, or the conditions under which
the story folk lived must be shown in such contrast to
the ones with which the child is familiar that they will
be very real to him. Take for instance the beginning
of the story of Joseph's coat told in this way:

"Long ago and in a far away land there lived a
father whose name was Jacob. He had a little son
named Joseph, and because the little boy needed a
home in which to live, food to eat, and clothes to wear
his father worked every day to get these things for
him. But Jacob did other things for his boy besides

work for him. Joseph needed to know what things were right for him to do, and how he could please God, his heavenly Father. These things his father taught him. As he grew older Jacob taught him also how to handle tools and do as much as a boy could of the work that needed to be done."

In this way a child like the child who hears the story is brought before him, one who has had the same struggles, the same effort to learn the things that little people must learn, and immediately the boy or girl to whom the tale is given feels a sense of kinship. Then, with his interest in the living, breathing Joseph aroused, how splendid is the incident of the beautiful coat, and how much enjoyed when they come to it in the story! This is a good rule to guide the inexperienced worker in amplifying a tale; supply enough details that are warranted to make the characters live under conditions sufficiently familiar to the children to make them feel kinship with them. Make the environment of the story people very like their own, or very unlike it, and emphasize the contrast. This sometimes necessitates considerable reading and study before one is equipped to supply the background. In order to amplify the Bible stories it means familiarity with the customs of Bible times, and not infrequently necessitates reading backward through many chapters to the very beginning of the thread of a story. But it pays, for without it many a story cannot be put into form that will deeply impress the children, and to tell a story, and feel with the telling that the children who hear it are drinking it in hungrily is one of the really gratifying things in life.

Analysis the first step in amplification.—Just as in condensing or rearranging a tale, in amplifying one we begin with an analysis and visualization of the plot. Then we proceed to clothe it, as the Frenchman said, so that all of its beauty and charm is accentuated. Determine what details are implied and then supply them so as to cover the skeleton and round it out in a complete, finished way. This does not mean supplying unwarranted fictitious details or interpolating matter that is irrelevant and serves no other purpose than to pad and lengthen the tale. It means introducing whatever, according to the laws of logic, must have occurred between the beginning of the story and the climax.

This is exactly what has been done in the amplification of the first three verses of the thirty-seventh chapter of Genesis. It is only logical to suppose that Israel must have shown to Joseph just the kind of solicitous love and care indicated. And whatever it is logical to suppose must have occurred, if it will make the pictures more vivid, may safely be introduced.

Take as an example the story of Mephibosheth, 2 Samuel 4. 4; 9. 1-13. Here is the plot outline of a gripping tale for children whose imaginations have begun to revel in fairy tale happenings, but which do not yet range far enough abroad that they can see details that are merely implied. The idea of a little boy whose father was a prince and whose grandfather was a king appeals to them instantly. It is but logical to suppose that for his day, Mephibosheth must have had the pretty things that in every period of history have been a part of the lot of children of royalty. Therefore why not supply such details as will make the child see him as he was, the loved scion of a line of kings? After the accident, and the discovery that the little prince had become lame, and had lost the beautiful home in which he had played so happily, sympathy is aroused to its highest pitch. And then how delightful it all is in the end, when he comes into his own again and is a prince in condition as well as in name and blood. No fairy tale is more appealing in the age of fairy tale lore than this narrative of the son of Jonathan.

This story may be handled in several ways. If the object of the teller is to emphasize the idea of God's care for his children, and to show how, through David's generosity, Mephibosheth comes into possession of all the things he had lost, the story would begin with a picture of the boy in the palace of his father.

A Little Lame Prince

Long, long ago, in a land far east of this, there was a little prince. His name was Mephibosheth, and he lived in a fine palace, for his father was a prince and his grandfather was a king, and very likely his mother was a princess. Everybody loved him, and he was happy in his beautiful home with all the pets a little boy could want and the curious toys that children of the East had in the days of long ago. Probably one of them was a tiny chariot, for there were no carriages or automobiles then and everybody who was rich enough to ride rode in a chariot, which looked something like a box open at the back and mounted upon two wheels. But when they were painted a bright, shining red and trimmed with gold flowers and bands and went speeding along behind fleet horses they looked very splendid, and kings took great pleasure in riding in chariots. So, of course, the little boys must have had toy chariots to play with, and probably Mephibosheth had several. And what a good time he must have had riding in them about the palace!

But one day a sad thing happened. His father and grandfather were killed in a war. People came running to the palace to tell the little boy's nurse about it, and they said that the soldiers who had killed the king and his son were coming to take the palace.

The good nurse was terribly frightened. Mephibosheth was only five years old, and she knew that with no father or grandfather to take care of him he might be hurt or killed. She loved him so much that she could not bear to think of any evil thing happening to him, and made up her mind to save him if she could.

"I will take him away to a safe place," she thought.

So she picked him up and started to run. She could hear the soldiers coming and wanted to get far from the palace before they reached it.

She ran and ran. Closer, closer came the soldiers, and faster, faster she hurried. She had almost reached a place where the little prince would be safe, and then —a dreadful thing happened. She dropped Mephibosheth on the hard, rough ground.

She did not mean to do it. She loved him and wanted to take care of him, you know. But when a boy is only five years old he is not big and strong. The fall hurt him terribly. It bruised his feet and legs and hurt him so much that it made him lame.

The poor nurse felt very sorry, and when the little boy cried, her heart ached as much as his feet did.

She picked him up again and hugged him close.

"My little Mephibosheth!" she said.

Then she ran on as fast as she could go.

By and by she came to a place where she knew he would be safe. There she stayed and kept him, and there the little boy grew into a big one. But his feet never got well again. He was always a lame prince, always one who had to go limping wherever he needed to go. He could not jump and run and play games like other boys. He could not swim in the cool water or do any of the things his strong young friends could do. When they had merry times he had to sit a little way off and watch them and wish that his own feet were straight and strong.

He did not have fine clothes any more, for when the soldiers took the palace they took all his father's money and pretty things too. Instead of being rich he was poor. Sometimes he did not have enough to eat to keep him from going hungry. He must have thought very often about the glad days when he lived in the palace and his father and grandfather were with him.

A long time passed. Then one day a lovely thing happened.

A very good king was ruling over the country. His name was David, and the people loved him. But David had not always been a king. Once he was a poor shepherd boy who had to stay in the hills and take care of his father's sheep. In the days when he watched over the gentle lambs he had learned to be kind and tender, and now that he was a great ruler he wanted to be the shepherd of his people as once he had been of his father's flocks. He tried to find a way of helping all who needed help.

King David had a servant who had worked in the palace of Prince Jonathan when Mephibosheth was a happy little boy, so, of course, he knew a great deal about everybody in the prince's family.

One day King David called this man and said to him, "Did Prince Jonathan have any sons or grandsons that I can show a kindness to?"

The servant answered, "Yes, Prince Jonathan left a son Mephibosheth, who is lame."

"Go and fetch him," the king said.

The servant went away from the palace, and a little while later when he came back, Mephibosheth was with him. The poor lame boy was very much frightened to hear that the king wanted to see him, and as he came limping into the great hall his face was white with fear.

"I hope he will not hurt me," he thought. He knew that he had done no wrong, yet sometimes in those far off days kings punished people who did not deserve it.

Do you think David was the kind of a king to do anything so wicked? No, indeed! He said to him: "I will give back to you all the lands and gold of your father, which the soldiers took away from you. For you must know that I loved your father very much."

Then for a moment King David sat very still and a sad look came into his face. He was thinking about Prince Jonathan and the happy days when they were young together.

"Yes, I loved him," he said, "and so I love you, his son. You shall live here in the palace with me. You shall sit beside me at the table and be even as my own son."

He told his servants to get fine clothes for Mephibosheth to wear and a gold chain to hang around his neck. He gave him a chariot and fleet horses, and whenever the lame prince drove through the streets of the city the people said, "See! The son of Prince Jonathan, whom David the king loves!"

So Mephibosheth was a happy prince once more, even though he was lame.

If the aim of the story-teller is to use this tale as one of a cycle of stories of David, the beginning may be with the picture of the king in an hour of loneliness in the palace dreaming of his boyhood among the sheep, of his friendship with Jonathan, and then lead back to the story of Jonathan's son. In that event the approach would be something like this:

David, the shepherd boy, who had watched his father's sheep, was a great king now. He lived in a palace and had chariots and horses, servants and houses and lands. But he still remembered the glad days among the hills of Bethlehem when he had played with the lambs. And very often, when he was alone, he sang the shepherd songs he used to sing as he led the flocks to green pastures. He thought, too, of his friend Prince Jonathan, King Saul's son, whom he had loved as a brother. Both Jonathan and his father were dead now, killed in battle on a hill called Gilboa.

"I wonder if Jonathan has any sons living that I can be kind to," David thought one day as he lived over the old times.

He called a servant who had once been with King Saul, and who knew all about the dead ruler's family. He told the man to tell him all he knew about them.

"Yes," the man answered, "Prince Jonathan has a son who is called Mephibosheth. He is lame, and lives in the house of a man named Machir.

"A lame son?" King David answered.

"Yes," the man said. "It is a sad story, how Mephibosheth came to have crippled feet. It happened the day Prince Jonathan and King Saul were killed. Mephibosheth was in the palace of his father with his nurse. When word came that the king and his son had fallen in battle this woman was very much afraid. She feared they might hurt the boy, for he was only five years old, and too little to take care of himself. So she picked him up and ran with him, for she wanted to get him to a safe place. But a very sad thing happened as she hurried along. She dropped him, and the fall hurt both his feet so much that it made him lame."

From this point continue the story as in the previous version and tell of David's sending for the son of Jonathan and give the succeeding events. It is obvious that the first version is the better one to use with beginners, because it contains direct discourse, and very young children can follow it more easily. Therefore they will like it better. In the latter part of the primary period, however, the second version will be enjoyed by them. It is well for the student to note what constitutes the difference between the two versions, and to bear in mind that direct discourse is the style of narrative in which all stories for very little children should be told. It is permissible for the story-teller to use indirect discourse in working with little children only when through some previously heard story they have become acquainted with the characters that are portrayed. Then, by beginning with one that has already become a friend, one may safely lead back from that character to some event. Soon after they come to Sunday school children learn to know David the shepherd boy, and will enjoy the story of Mephibosheth even though it is given as supplementary to that of the greatest of Hebrew kings.

From these examples it will be seen that many an incident may be amplified into a tale for telling if implied details are supplied. But only that which it is logical to suppose *must* have occurred should be introduced.

Another of the many incidents from the Bible that can be amplified into a very lovely story for the child is that of Onesimus in the epistle of Paul to Philemon,

the tale of a slave in Colossæ who steals some of the
belongings of his master and flees to Rome. There,
through the eloquence of Paul the apostle, he is con-
verted to Christianity and comes to be very much loved
by Paul. With regeneration accomplished by the word
of Jesus comes an eagerness to make restitution to the
master he has robbed. He returns to Philemon, no
longer the embittered bondman, but the submissive,
willing servant. And as he goes he bears a letter from
the apostle beseeching Philemon to receive him "as a
brother beloved."

In this incident we find all the elements of a story,
one that will lead the child to see the futility of attempting to shirk obligations, the transforming power
of the Christ in a life, and the splendid tolerance and
charity of Paul. The picture of the slave to whom
life was hard and gray will immediately awaken a feeling of pity, if that slave is brought before the children
like a creature of flesh and blood. He might be introduced in this way:

In a far away land a long, long time ago, there lived
a man who was a slave. A slave is a person who belongs to another, just as his dog or cow belongs to him,
who must work day in and day out and never get any
pay for his work, no matter how much he does. It
is very hard to be a slave, for slaves are nearly
always tired, and they never have nice homes, pretty
clothes, or good things to eat.

One day this slave was looking at the beautiful things
that belonged to his master. There were sacks of
money, gold and silver dishes, diamonds and all kinds
of jewels, and splendid clothes.

"How I wish they were mine!" he thought.

Once a clear picture is painted of the slave, the conditions under which he lived and his deep longing for freedom and a happier life, his career will be followed with eager interest, and it is easy to carry the child along with him through the flight to Rome, the conversion there and the return to Colossæ, and to impress upon him as he listens the great lesson the narrative teaches.

If this story is intended for beginners, it should be made short and simple, a bare outline of the plot and sufficient explanatory touches to delineate the characters being all that should be attempted, the theory being that the younger the children the less complex should be the narratives given to them. With primary pupils there can be more comprehensive explanatory and atmospheric touches and a more delicate etching of the pictures. For them this incident works well into a series of stories about Onesimus, the divisions of which would be as follows:

1. The Slave Who Ran Away.
2. Onesimus and the Good Teacher.
3. The Return of the Runaway.

In order to develop a series of stories considerable elaboration is necessary, but this does not mean that there is to be padding that serves no other purpose than to lengthen the tale. The condensed version for beginners requires only that the plot thread, personages, and conditions be made clear. In the series a detailed picture can be painted of the country in which Onesimus lived, of the plight of the slave there, the contrasting luxury and comfort of the master, the deep

envy of the bondman and his yearning for liberty.
In the account of Onesimus and Paul some idea should
be given of Rome in its magnificence, the wickedness
of the people, and the simplicity and beauty of life of
the men of the early Christian Church, that gleams
against the corruption like a white flame of purifica-
tion. And after the children have seen the redemp-
tion of the thief and the rebellious slave turned will-
ingly submissive, they should see the affectionate fare-
well of the apostle and the departure of Onesimus
from the Eternal City by the ship that will carry
him back to the shore from whence he fled.

Thus it will be seen that by supplying details that are
implied many an incident may be amplified into a story
for telling. But the student should remember that this
means only that which it is logical to suppose must
have happened or have been the condition under which
the character or characters lived. It does not mean
license to introduce unwarranted fictitious details.
The skeleton of the plot indicated, it is not difficult to
round it out, for one needs only to visualize the setting and characters and portray them as he sees them,
and to interpolate something of the conversation that is
likely to have occurred. This suggests itself once we
have come to see and to feel the pictures. Dialogue is
a very great aid in making situations vivid and characters alive to the child. Therefore the story-teller
should not be parsimonious about employing it freely,
either in amplification or in simple retelling.

If the imagination is called into full play, if the visualizing has been clear before one attempts any am-

plification, it is not difficult to develop well-rounded and well-proportioned stories from bare outlines. What must have been the condition of life of Philemon? What were the possessions of prosperous men in the land of Phrygia in those days? What must have been the thoughts of the slave in seeing and feeling the contrast between their positions? What must have been the emotional effect upon Onesimus when his conversion gave him finer ideals and beliefs than those he had held, and he realized he was a thief and malefactor? What must have been the attitude of Paul, the apostle of Him whose creed was love and forgiveness, upon learning the remorse of the slave and the conditions that had caused him to sin? The measure of success in elaborating this or any other story depends upon the free *play of the imagination* and the vividness with which one can see the slave, the master, the Phrygian land, Rome, the place of corruption and splendor, and the glorified follower of Jesus who was working there. This will entail considerable reference work. It means consulting a history of Rome of the days of Paul for a clear picture of Rome. It means reading at least an encyclopædia account of Phrygia, the country in which Colossæ was located, and in getting a definite idea of the setting of the tale. It requires time and effort, but the labor of preparing the material melts into insignificance beside satisfaction in the results obtained, and the willingness to do it differentiates the artist from the indifferent and slipshod craftsman.

Thought Questions

1. Why is the ability to amplify material necessary to the story-teller?

2. Why is it necessary to supply whatever is implied in telling stories to little children?

3. What is the first step in amplification?

4. What difference should there be between stories intended for beginners and those for primary pupils?

5. Upon what does success in amplification depend?

Assignment

Prepare for telling to children in the Primary Department the story of Onesimus, making the incident as given in Philemon the basis of a series of three stories.

Prepare for telling to beginners the story of Abram Giving Lot the First Choice, Genesis 13. 5-11.

CHAPTER VIII

PRACTICE IN BEGINNINGS, CLIMAXES, AND ENDINGS

Variety in beginnings.—The creative artist is a versatile individual, a personage who is not hampered by one form of execution or medium of expression. Mastery of many strokes and lines gives the painter facility to portray upon canvas whatever scenes or figures formalize in his mind, so that if he visions a shepherd with his flocks and dogs it is not beyond his power to create that shepherd because he knows how to draw only horses. Likewise the writer can etch his word pictures in numerous different forms, and the story-teller who is worthy of the name must be able to introduce and sustain his narrative in various ways and not be restricted by one stock tale as a model upon which all tales must be constructed. Even little children quickly discover if the mother or teacher always tells stories in the same way and welcome a narrator who has something different. Proof of this fact was given to me several years ago when an Indian story was told to a group of seven-year-olds. It was the twenty-third of February, and knowing they had heard anecdotes of George Washington and that they had made hatchet and cherry-tree posters, the story-teller began, "Before your great-great-grandmother was born, so long ago that George Washington was just a tiny baby and didn't know a cherry tree from a bunch of clover." As the tale was finished a grunt of satisfaction came from a little brown-eyed fellow, who exclaimed: "My, but that was a nice story! Teacher don't know any but long, long-ago ones."

A beginning different from the accustomed one had increased his pleasure in the narrative, for although we do not always realize it, children are very exacting critics. They are quite as quick as adults to prefer the story-teller who uses a variety of beginnings to the one whose yarns are always introduced in the same way. "Once upon a time," and "Long, long ago," are magical words to a child, but so are "In the days of long ago." "There was once a beautiful valley," "Far away across the ocean lived a boy named Hans," and a dozen other clauses the skillful narrator can use for her introductory one. Let the children see that you have more than one way of opening a story and you will become in their eyes a more wonderful person than she who, as the little boy said, "knows only long, long-ago ones."

The best guide for practice in beginnings is a copy of Grimm, Andersen, Perrault, Bechstein, or any other collection of folk tales. Cast as these are in a form that is as appealing now as it was in the early morning of the world, they are models of story openings that will grip a child. Take, for instance, these from a collection of Russian folk tales:

"In a certain country there lived an old couple who had a daughter named Marusia." "Once there was an old man who was such an awful drunkard as passes all description." "A bad wife lived on the worst of terms with her husband and never paid any attention to what he said." "A certain woman was very bumptious." "In a little village there was a rich merchant named Marko, and a stingier fellow never lived." "In the olden years long, long ago, there came upon the world distress and shame."

Any collection of folk tales will offer a large variety of beginnings, and the greater the versatility of the narrator in opening his stories the more pronounced will his success be.

Follow the study of beginnings of masterpieces in the general field with an observation of openings of Bible stories, and consider how effectively theme, characters, and locality are introduced in these: "There was a man named Zacchæus, which was chief among the publicans, and he was rich"; "There was in a city a judge which feared not God, neither regarded man"; "And it came to pass, on the second Sabbath after the first, that he went through the corn fields, and his disciples plucked the ears of corn and did eat, rubbing them in their hands"; "And it came to pass after these things, that Naboth the Jezreelite had a vineyard, which was in Jezreel, hard by the palace of Ahab, King of Samaria"; "And he removed from thence unto a mountain on the east of Bethel, and pitched his tent, having Bethel on the west and Hai on the east; and there he builded an altar unto the Lord."

"And it came to pass, in the ninth year of his reign,

in the tenth month, in the tenth day of the month, that Nebuchadnezzar king of Babylon came, he, and all his host, against Jerusalem, and pitched against it; and they built forts against it round about" (2 Kings 25. 1).

A modernized beginning for this Bible story would be:

"A king named Zedekiah was ruling over the land of Judah, and in the ninth year of his reign Nebuchadnezzar, King of Babylon, came with an army to make war upon him. He set his soldiers around the city of Jerusalem and built forts upon every side."

Introducing characters and setting in beginnings. —To begin a story so it catches and holds the interest of the audience requires more than versatility in the opening sentence. Added to this must be ability to introduce in the first paragraph the characters, or some of them, to give an idea of the traits of one or more of them, or to set a problem around which the tale is built. This is done in all the childhood favorites, "Red Riding Hood," "Cinderella," "Sleeping Beauty," and the great company of fairy narratives. It is done in the works of Josephus, in the immortal legends of the Middle Ages, in the Bible, and in every other piece of literature that has been a power among people who were children at heart, and to which the masters of to-day are going for help in their efforts to reach the child consciousness. Note this beginning of a popular Muscovite tale:

"A bad wife lived on the worst of terms with her husband and never paid any attention to what he said.

If he told her to get up early she would lie in bed three days at a stretch. If he wanted her to go to sleep she couldn't think of sleeping, and when he asked her to make pancakes she would say, 'You clown, you don't deserve a pancake.' "

A very clear conception of the character of the wife is obtained from this one paragraph, and immediately the mind of the hearer sets to working and wondering about what will happen to this bad and stubborn woman.

From the eleventh chapter of the ninth book of Josephus we have, "Now when Zechariah, the son of Jeroboam, had reigned six months over Israel, he was slain by the treachery of a certain friend of his, whose name was Shallu, the son of Jabesh, who took the kingdom afterward but kept it no more than thirty days." Here, again, interest arises with the opening sentence and immediately the hearer wonders, "Why did he keep it only thirty days?"

Likewise in the Bible story of Hezekiah, 2 Kings 20. 1, we find the following introduction of characters in the first paragraph:

"In those days was Hezekiah sick unto death. And the prophet Isaiah, the son of Amoz, came to him and said unto him, Thus saith the Lord. Set thine house in order, for thou shalt die, and not live."

Principles involved in beginnings.—One might add indefinitely to the list of model beginnings and find the same principles involved in every one of them:

(1) The introductory phrase that gives a vivid word picture of either time or characters.

(2) The setting of a problem or the involving of characters in conflict.

In "The King of the Golden River" the problem is set in the first paragraph with the statement that Gluck was happy-hearted and kind, whereas Hans and Schwartz were so cruel and stingy that they were known all about as "The Black Brothers."

In the Bible story of Jonah, the problem is set in the first paragraph:

"Now the word of the Lord came unto Jonah, the son of Amittai, saying, Arise, go to Nineveh, that great city, and cry against it! for their wickedness is come up before me."

In the story of Christ and the Lord's Prayer the problem is set in the first paragraph:

"And it came to pass, that as he was praying in a certain place, one of his disciples said unto him, Lord, teach us to pray, as John also taught his disciples to pray." And then Jesus helps them to overcome their difficulty.

No matter how many stories we study we find that a problem or element of conflict is introduced with the beginning of the plot thread, and practice in opening stories so as to achieve this result in the first paragraph is a necessary part of the narrator's preparation.

Practice in writing beginnings.—After practicing beginnings of retold stories the student should write the beginnings of several original ones, even if he has no idea of ever telling them, and several beginnings to the same story. This practice will give increased facility in opening the retold tale and enable him to bring his characters upon the stage the moment the curtain is lifted. The more original work one does the better fitted he is to pass on the value of stories that have grown with the race, for by his own efforts to create he will come into a deeper appreciation of the perfection of tales that had their origin in deep longing and desire. More than one student who at first regarded original work as something necessary only for those who aspired to become writers has expressed gratitude for a training in something that was once considered irksome, because out of original work had come power to *recreate* instead of just to *repeat* the stories found in books.

Analysis of climaxes.—For practice in climaxes a like study should be made of the climaxes of great stories. In what does the climax of each tale lie?

In Hans Christian Andersen's "Ugly Duckling" the climax is in the discovery that the persecuted little creature is a beautiful white swan. In "Tarpeia," as retold by Sara Cone Bryant in *How to Tell Stories for Children,* it lies in the part beginning, "The soldier lifted high his left arm. 'Take thy reward,' he said, and as he spoke he hurled upon her that which he wore upon it. Down upon her head crashed—not the silver rings of the soldier, but the great brass shield he carried in battle."

In the "Story of Jairus's Daughter" the climax is contained in the paragraph where Jesus comes to the house, sends the strangers away and says to the mourning family, "She is not dead; she sleepeth."

In the story of Belshazzar's feast the climax lies in

the last words of the interpretation of Daniel, "God hath numbered thy kingdom and finished it," cto. (Daniel 5. 26, 27, 28.)

The climax of a story is the revealment of a secret. It is the moment of discovery, the sudden straightening of a tangled thread. Because the conflict in the story has awakened expectation in the minds of the hearers the climax is dramatic—unless it is spoiled and weakened by crude handling on the part of the teller. The climax must be expressed in simple language without any attempt at high-sounding style. In a word, it should be given in something of the manner in which a child tells a secret to another child. An analysis of climaxes of masterpieces shows that this is exactly what is done by all great artists in the field of narration, and the more closely the beginner studies these the more confident he can be of success.

Necessity of practice.—Follow the analytical study and practice in giving the climaxes of old stories with work on original ones, always with the aim of improving upon each succeeding effort. This is what differentiates the artist from the amateur, this painstaking care and infinite attention to detail. There are those who object, "But working a story over kills life and destroys spontaneity!" Instead, it does just the opposite, and tales that seem to have been reeled off are often the sixth, tenth or twelfth revision. Jean Webster's "Daddy Long Legs" sounds like the babbling of a naïve girl, but Jean Webster's waste basket was filled and refilled many times as the first, second, and third versions were discarded. Fannie Hurst, often called "the female O. Henry," is one of the most painstaking of authors, sometimes spending an entire day in writing and recasting a single paragraph. Mary Austin devoted seven years to writing *The Land of Little Rain,* and Booth Tarkington, Mary Roberts Rinehart, and many other famous writers attest to the necessity of revision and more revision. And what the skilled professional finds necessary the amateur cannot afford to neglect. She needs to practice upon the construction of beginnings, climaxes, and endings and the manner of giving them to the child, both the original stories she may not tell and the world-old ones she certainly will relate.

A girl who has had remarkable success as a storyteller made a scrapbook of three sections, into one of which she pasted model beginnings which she clipped from magazine stories and old books; in another model climaxes, and in a third model endings. She copies these parts from such stories as "Red Riding Hood," "The Ugly Duckling," "Cinderella," and whenever she finds occasion to construct or adapt material to fit her needs she goes to her scrapbook for inspiration and guidance, then writes the story, compares the parts that are so vital with the model ones, and revises and recasts her own work in conformity with the same.

"It is my treasure house," she said not long ago in speaking of it, "and as long as I tell stories I cannot afford to be without it."

Ending the story.—Ending a story means nothing more than rounding out and finishing it, once the climax has been reached, so that it does not sound

abrupt and incomplete. Some stories end logically
with the climax and the addition of another sentence
tends to blur the picture that should be the final one
before the vision. *The Last Lesson* of Alphonse
Daudet is a good example of a tale of this type, the
climax being in the words, "And then he wrote high
up in big letters, 'Vive la France!'

"And he made a little sign with his head, 'That is
all. Go away!' "

In the Bible story of Belshazzar's feast, the ending
is thus:

"In that night was Belshazzar the king of the Chal-
deans slain and Darius the Median took the kingdom."

In some stories that end in the climax a sentence of
recapitulation completes the narrative in a manner
pleasing to the child. "And they say that is why the
sea is salt." "And that is why the morning glory
climbs."

Disposing of characters.—Sometimes, even after
the climax is reached, there are characters that must
be disposed of, and in this event the ending consists of
such sentences or paragraphs as will remove them
speedily from the scene but not abruptly, using no more
words than are necessary to do it.

"So Tarpeia lay buried beneath the reward she
claimed, and the Sabines marched past her dead body
into the city she had betrayed."

The story of the Baby Jesus, as prepared by Miss
Danielson,[1] ends simply and impressively with: "The

---

[1] International Closely Graded Lessons. Beginner's Teacher's Text Book
Part I, Lesson 11.

shepherds looked and wondered. They told the angels' good news and the song in the sky. All that heard it wondered. Mary never forgot what the shepherds said. Often she thought of it—the angels' good news and the song in the sky. And the shepherds went back to their sheep, thanking God for his gift of the little Lord Jesus in his crib lined with hay."

It is necessary to dispose of the shepherds in this way, in order to bring the story to a logical ending, for the children, knowing they came from the hills, will wonder if they stayed by the manger or if they went back to their flocks, which they left untended, and without being told whether they did or not will experience a sense of incompleteness. If in doubt as to this tell the Christmas story to a group of little children without giving this final touch and see how quickly they will ask what the shepherds did then.

Note these simple, but wonderfully effective, endings of Bible stories:

"And he dwelt in the wilderness of Paran and his mother took him a wife out of the land of Egypt."

"So David went his way, and Saul returned to his place."

"And the field and the cave that is therein were made sure unto Abraham for a possession of a burying place, by the sons of Heth."

"And Isaac brought her unto his mother Sarah's tent, and took Rebekah, and she became his wife; and he loved her; and Isaac was comforted after his mother's death."

"And they went forth and preached everywhere, the

Lord working with them, and confirming the word with signs following."

"And no man was able to answer him a word; neither durst any man from that day forth ask him any more questions."

The teller of Bible stories will find that if he keeps very closely to the Bible endings, his efforts will be crowned with success. Often it is necessary to modernize the wording, but the thought expressed should be that of the Hebrew story-tellers expressed in terms that the child can understand. To improve upon the dramatic beauty of style of these old-time narrators is something we of to-day cannot hope to accomplish. Therefore let the child have as nearly as possible the Bible version in beginnings, climaxes, and endings which are without a parallel in literary artistry.

Summary.—Summing up, the ending should consist in removing the characters from the scene after the climax has been reached, in a sentence of recapitulation, or with the climax itself if the action logically terminates there, using only what is necessary to round out the tale and make it seem complete. It is a mistake to pad an oral story anywhere, but to pad the ending is fatal to the future success of the narrator with that same group of hearers, because by lengthening it unnecessarily he mars their pleasure in it. A child likes to let his imagination play freely about a tale he has just heard, and for the narrator to go rambling on to no purpose makes that flight of fancy impossible for him. The ideal way is to allow him a few minutes of silence, five if possible, after the completion of each

story, to live again in its scenes and touch hands with
its characters. But where this is not possible, where a
discussion must follow the story and the time for it is
limited, at least make a short pause, so that he may
realize the story is finished, but do not continue talking when he feels that you have finished and wonders
why you do not stop.

The same sort of study of endings of classic stories
should be made that is made of beginnings and
climaxes, keeping the above stated principles in mind.
And later these principles and the result of the observation should be applied to original work. Thus
the story-teller grows into a power that in the beginning he believed he could never acquire and becomes
deservedly a member of that splendid company, many
of which are nameless in history, but who shaped
tribal ideals and molded nations.

Thought Questions

1. Why is ability to use variety of beginnings necessary to the story-teller?

2. What are the principles involved in beginnings?

3. Of what advantage is practice in writing beginnings, climaxes, and endings?

4. What is the principle involved in making the
climax effective to the child?

5. What are the principles involved in ending a
story?

Assignment

Prepare for telling to Primary pupils the story of
Herod's malicious intent toward the child Jesus.
Matthew 2.

Write *three* different beginnings for the story.
Write *three* different climaxes.
Write *three* different endings.

Prepare in the same way for Beginners the story of Jesus feeding the multitude.   John 6. 1-13.

CHAPTER IX

PRACTICE IN THE DEVELOPMENT OF A SPECIFIC TRUTH

Emphasizing truth by amplification.—Sometimes it is necessary to illuminate the specific characteristic or truth that is the motive of the story, to emphasize it even more forcibly than it is emphasized in the written narrative, in order that it may be more completely grasped by the child. This is especially so in dealing with little people whose habits of action we wish to reconstruct, as, for instance, the untruthful child, the selfish, cruel, or lazy child, the boy or girl who is slovenly, inattentive, or habitually impolite. It is possible to tell a story and tell it so entertainingly that children will be held by it without catching its lesson or purpose if to the narrator herself that lesson does not stand out as the salient feature of the tale. And sometimes even when she appreciates fully its aim and meaning, because she assumes that the children understand more than they do, they do not realize its underlying truth. Therefore ability to stress that truth so forcibly that it stays with the child long after he has left the teller, and at the same time to do it so artistically that there is no sense of being preached to, is one of the fundamentals of all story-telling whose aim is ethical and constructive. The narrator must know how to bring out the high lights of a story with a few skillful strokes as the painter brings out those of his picture, being never the preacher to the boy or girl but always the magic conductor who leads him into fascinating regions.

Emphasizing by repetition.—Repetition is one of the best devices for making emphatic the message we wish the child to receive.

In the old story of "The Boy Who Cried 'Wolf,' " which is one of the best tales for giving a realization of the inevitable suffering that comes of untruthfulness, some elaboration of the part in which the men refuse to go to aid of the lad who had deceived them twice will make it apparent why the boy had to suffer. The original tale gives the bare facts:

Then one day the wolf did come. "Help! Help!" the boy cried, "A wolf! A wolf!"

But the men would not go.

"He is at his tricks again," they said.

The wolf ran in among the flock and killed many of the sheep.

A version that stresses the fact that misfortune came to the boy because of having deceived before would read something like this:

Then one day the wolf did come.

"Help! Help!" the boy cried. "The wolf! The wolf!"

Over in the field beyond the woodchoppers heard him, but they did not even stop to listen.

"He is at his tricks again," said one of them.

"Yes, he has fooled us twice," said another. "We will not let him do it again."

He called and called, "Help! Help! The wolf! The wolf!"

But the men went right on chopping wood.

"Let him shout as much as he pleases," they said. "We will not go again."

And they did not go.

The wolf ran in among the flock and killed many of the sheep.

With the lesson emphasized in this manner during the unrolling of the plot the child understands what may come of untruthfulness, and it is not necessary to moralize in concluding the tale and say, "And that shows what happens to boys and girls who do not tell the truth." Occasionally a closing sentence of this kind is permissible. Children enjoy it as the finale of some humorous tales, but it is not so with serious ones. They do not care what the story-teller thinks. They are interested only in knowing what happens, and a little repetition or elaboration as the plot thread unrolls will often bring an emotional awakening that the most carefully worded maxims cannot do.

In the story of manna sent to the children of Israel the lesson to be left with the child is of God's care of them. Here is a good example of what is meant by emphasis by amplification:

Moses heard the words of God, and then he called the Israelites together that he might tell them what he had said.

"Have no fear," he spoke, "for at evening ye shall know that God is taking care of you. And in the morning ye shall see what great things Jehovah hath done."

The people watched and waited. When evening came they knew that what Moses had said was true, for they saw large flocks of birds called quail. Quail are good for food when they are cooked. The Israelites caught as many as they thought they should need, prepared them for eating, and had all the food they wanted that night.

In the morning dew that was bright and shining lay around their tents. When the sun came out it went away, and after it was gone small, round things were seen upon the ground. They were white and looked like tiny pieces of bread.

Moses said to them, "Behold, it is the bread which Jehovah hath given you to eat. Gather ye of it as much as ye want."

At first they could not believe it was bread, for never before had anyone heard of bread falling from the sky. But when they tasted some of the tiny bits they found them sweet as honey and very good to eat.

They called them manna. And as they ate they thanked God with all their hearts.

Morning after morning they found the manna upon the ground, and gathered it for their food. They were not hungry any more, and they were not afraid. They knew God was taking care of them.

In the story of the contributions for the tabernacle, Exodus 35, the lesson of the willingness of the donors can be stressed by repetition.

The words of Moses made all of them willing-hearted, and they brought the most precious things they had that they might help in building the house of

God. The girls and women gave their bracelets, earrings, and jewels of gold. Every man that had blue, purple, or scarlet cloth gave it as part of his share. They brought goat's hair, ram's skins dyed red, acacia wood, and silver and brass. They gave onyx stones, spice, and oil and sweet perfume. Nobody had thought they could gather together so many beautiful things.

Emphasis by contrast.—In the "Story of the Baby Jesus" the salient truth is joyful thanks for God's best gift, and the high light of the tale is the singing of the angels, because this sounds the note of gratitude and jubilation. As given in the book of Luke the tale is exquisite and perfect, and needs no touch to illuminate it for the older children or for the adult. But it has been my experience that the tiny child of average intelligence and sensitiveness does not grasp the underlying thought unless this portion is emphasized and amplified. He understands the Babe in the manger and the mother because mothers and babies are a part of his own experience. But his idea of the celestial singers is vague and confused unless the story-teller introduces them in terms he understands. This does not mean to describe the angels, to attribute to them yellow hair or blue eyes or to picture what should be left to the free play of the fancy. It means to give an idea of the dazzling brightness and splendor the shepherds glimpsed on the Nativity night, and to stress the music of the heavenly choir so that the child hears it as he hears many another sound that is never voiced in words. As given by one narrator the description of the singing of the angels is as follows: "And all at

once the sky was filled with angels, singing. And this was their song:
"Glory to God in the highest,
And on earth peace among men in whom he is well
    pleased.
"Then the song ended, and the light faded, and the shepherds were left alone in the quiet and the darkness. They were left alone, excited and wondering over the good news the angel had brought."

Stressing the brightness and splendor of the singing hosts that was followed by all the night blackness and stillness makes the contrast strong to the child and heightens the note of joy for him, and he begins to comprehend the gladness of the shepherds as they hurried to Bethlehem. To the child who is still in the rhythmical period repetition of bits of song and dialogue adds intensely to his interest in and understanding of the story, and this repetition means as much in the Bible tales as it means in folk tales like "Jack and the Bean-stalk" and "Nimmy Nimmy Not." The story-teller should bear in mind, when he uses repetition in Bible narratives, that the written version of any great tale is for reading, and that to recast it for that purpose would be license. But for telling, in order to bring vivid pictures and keen enjoyment to the hearer, the high lights must often be illuminated, and whenever he employs amplification and repetition for this purpose, whenever he introduces only what is *implied,* he is acting within his province as an artist. The great narrators of long ago did this constantly, and those remarkable but unsung artists, the strolling

story-tellers of Sicily and Calabria, are doing it to this
day. As a child I had heard from a teacher at school
the account of the boy Garibaldi running away to become a sailor. As a woman I heard the same plot on
a street corner of Mongerbino from the lips of old
Gulielmo Bondi as he entertained the street boys one
afternoon when it was too hot to work and they
crowded in the shadow of a shopdoor seeking shelter
from the sirocco. But it was not the same story, although the Sicilian did not interpolate a single unwarranted incident into the life tale of the patriot. He
used the very ones used by the teacher who told the
story as she found it in a book. But he did illuminate
the high lights, and by doing this he made the romance
as vivid to the boys who heard it as if they themselves
had lived through some of the experiences.

In the story of the coming of the Magi amplification
will aid the teacher in impressing upon the child the
truth that love is the best gift, and the quality of the
love that lay back of the visit of the Wise Men of the
East.

The Wise Men had traveled miles and miles across
the sands on their camels just to give these presents to
the little Lord Jesus. They had forded rivers that
were so swift and deep the camels had to swim across,
and sometimes it had seemed they must surely be
drowned. They had climbed mountains where the
roads were steep and rough, and they had risked
danger of every kind that they might lay their gifts
before him. For the Lord Jesus was not a common
baby. He had come to be the Prince of Peace and to

make people happier and better. He had come to save
the world.

Thus the underlying truth of every story one tells
can be brought home to the child. Thus, through
skillful amplification and repetition by the narrator he
will come into a realization of its meaning and message that he might not gain without it.

Whoever tells stories of the Christ-Child will gain
much inspiration for her work by a careful study of
Ben Hur. In this book a man with a great soul has
told reverently and vividly of the shepherds on the
hills, the Babe in the manger, and the coming of the
Wise Men, and to read it is to see with clearer eyes
than one has seen before the Bethlehem hills and the
glory that came upon them on the Nativity night. In
fact, wherever artists have recounted the old stories
of the east, the teller of Bible narratives should go for
help in her work, for by reading or hearing the account of men who have sensed completely their meaning and beauty is to gain a deeper understanding of the
most wonderful of all tales, and through that understanding to give more to the child. Therefore the
works of Lew Wallace, Henry van Dyke, John of
Hildesheim, Selma Lagerlof, and those other masters
who have written of days and deeds in Palestine
should be a part of the equipment of every one who
aspires to acquaint children with the oldest and best
of books.

THOUGHT QUESTIONS

1. In what *three* ways may the specific truth of a
story be stressed or emphasized?

2. Illustrate with some story how the emphasis can be made by repetition; by amplification; by contrast.

Assignment

Emphasize the truth involved in each of the following stories:

The Duty of Obedience, Genesis 2. 16-25; 3. 1-24.

Love Shown by Kindness, Luke 10. 30-35.

Obedience to the Will of God, Joshua 1. 1-6; 3. 4, 5. 10-12.

CHAPTER X

THE CHILD'S USE OF STORIES

Forms of expression.—The child's spontaneous expression of a story holds almost as much delight for him as the first hearing held, because thereby he re-experiences the thrills and wonderment its scenes awakened. And until the teacher follows each narrative with a period in which such free expression can be made she does not realize the power of the spoken tale as an awakener of moods and molder of ideals.

This expression may be of various forms, such as playing the story, singing, drawing, cutting and modeling it, or acting it in pantomime, and with children of artistic temperament and keen intelligence is often wholly spontaneous. There is no such thing as hearing a tale without some reaction toward it, but a majority of children need leadership before they will express that reaction. Under sympathetic leadership, however, the emotions the scenes have aroused will be manifested, and this manifestation is of utmost value to the child, for each additional experience with the tale fixes the basic truths more deeply. Moreover, as Sara Cone Bryant says, the child's spontaneous expression of a story helps to set free his natural creative impulses, and in this field alone the art of the narrator has a great mission to perform. Too many people are like "The Voiceless Singers" of Oliver Wendell Holmes, who "die with all their music in them." And when one looks over the history of artistic attainment and notes that the lands in which the fine arts have flowered most splendidly are those where, for centuries, story-telling has had an honored place, it is not illogical to think that with a more serious and general use of stories among children there may be fewer voiceless folk in the future.

Pantomime and singing.—Very little children delight in impersonating some of the characters in pantomime. This is the first step toward dramatization, and dramatization, properly guided and controlled, is as valuable in the Sunday school as in the day school. Through playing a story the child lives to the uttermost the experiences of that story, and therefore the lessons it teaches are stamped upon his memory in an unforgettable way. Some little folk are remarkably expressive and resourceful when it comes to playing the story, and will portray its happenings in a swift, unbroken sequence without suggestion from the teacher or leader, capably and joyfully creating each part. Others, as some one has said, are limited by nature. Yet these slow, inexpressive little people derive just as much joy and benefit from dramatization as their more facile and temperamental companions, provided they are under the leadership of one who, by skillful direction, can awaken their dormant activities and free them from the chains of diffidence. For them pantomime dramatization is an easy, almost spontaneous form of expression, because it makes possible the play experience of the story without the embarrassment that comes of not knowing what to say. In the Beginners' Department it is advisable to attempt only pantomime dramatization, and at first but one of the scenes or incidents of the tale. And this should be the one of the children's choice, the one that to them stands out as the salient feature of the story. I recall a group of beginners who, after hearing about David the Shepherd, took keen delight in a march of a shepherd and sheep. Then the teacher suggested that it would be nice to have a song about David to sing as they marched, and out of many suggestions from the class and the guiding mind of the teacher behind the suggestion, of which, however, the children were unaware, a little song was "made up" that ran like this:

> David was a shepherd boy,
> David was a shepherd boy,
> David was a shepherd boy,
> And he loved his sheep.

Da - vid was a shepherd boy, Da - vid was a shepherd boy,

Da - vid was   a shep-herd boy, And   he loved his sheep.

> In the pastures green and sweet, (repeat)
> David watched them feed.

Came a lion fierce and wild,   (repeat)
    To the tender sheep.

David drove the beast away,   (repeat)
    Shepherd good was he.

The number of stanzas may be increased to tell the complete story of David, for children love the repetition of line and rhythm. An attempt at rhyme is unnecessary, even unwise, for the songs little people have a hand in creating must be marked by many crudities, and to undertake to polish them to anything like the standard of an adult production is to rob them of life and of joy for the child. The tiny boy or girl is like the primitive Indian or Negro on the Southern plantation of ante-bellum days, and his very own songs react his thoughts and feelings. They must be *his* form of expression instead of highly finished productions that are fitted down to him. It is imperative that the teacher's attitude toward these crude, spontaneous forms of expression be one of sympathetic understanding, that she shall not expect too much and by attempts at pruning and polishing kill enthusiasm and creative joy. And I know of no better way in which she may obtain an understanding of about what to expect of very young children in a creative way than to study some of the Indian tribal songs and religious hymns of the Negroes, because the people among whom these formalized were a child people. The publications of the American Folklore Society are rich in material from both races, and I recommend especially the songs of the Fisk Jubilee Singers, which may be obtained in any of the larger public libraries.

It is sometimes advisable for the teacher to begin the little song, work out the first stanza, for instance. Any teacher can do this, because a single line used in repetition will comprise a stanza, and somewhere among her stock of melodies is one to which she can fit the words. The imitative instinct of the children will cause them to suggest other lines, and so as a class production, the stanzas grow and the story is told. And it is well to remember that the exterior crudity that marks the production is attended on the part of the child with inner perceptions of extreme delicacy and fineness. And because of these perceptions the boy or girl who has worked out in his own unfinished way a song play of David the Shepherd is better fitted to understand the Good Shepherd and his care than one who has had no such play.

Whether in pantomime or oral, dramatization should be the child's expression. Therefore the teacher should not work out the story in her own way and tell him what to do. But suggestions and leadership are necessary, for without them children who are shy or are limited in creative impulse will give little or no response to this valuable form of expression. Suppose the story has been told of Mephibosheth and David. After the children have talked of the good king and the lame boy the teacher says, "Suppose we play the story? Who wants to be little Mephibosheth?"

Immediately somebody will volunteer because every child knows how to impersonate a lame child.

"Who will be the nurse?"

(The children will make the discovery that probably the teacher will have to be the nurse because none of them are large enough to carry Mephibosheth.)

"Who wants to be King David? The servant? Mephibosheth, what are you going to do?"

The child himself will suggest and the other children will suggest actions in keeping with the part. By questioning, draw them out as to what should be the action of the various characters, the children demonstrating the same, and after a little impersonation of this kind they will put the story together and play it with a surprising degree of spontaneity. Although the teacher's suggestions have made it possible, it will still be their portrayal, and they will enter into it with an abandon that will not be possible if they are told what to do and where to do it.

Drawing, Coloring, and Paper Cutting.—Almost every worker with little children knows the value of drawing the story by the child, of coloring pictures that illustrate it, and of cutting freehand silhouette outlines of its personages and objects. Every one of these forms of expression requires the visualizing of each image portrayed, and the cutting and freehand drawing are especially valuable in developing the power of conceiving and holding the concrete image of the idea given, and therefore tend directly to increase creative ability.

Under no condition, however, should the teacher look upon handiwork as purely occupational, or as something to keep the children out of mischief. Drawing, coloring, and paper cutting are highly valuable when they are an expression by the child of some idea the story has awakened in him. In that event they are constructive, upbuilding forces. But when the teacher regards them as something to keep the children quiet they become what one worker calls "busy idleness" and are harmful in their effect because they get the children into the habit of doing something to no purpose. The same punctilious care on the part of the teacher that makes possible a spontaneous piece of dramatization, the same constructive suggestion and questioning must be the foundation upon which all handwork in the church school is built. Otherwise it should not be employed.

Modeling.—Where space is limited it is not always possible to use the sand table. But there is no classroom so small as to prohibit the use of antiseptic modeling clay such as is prepared for children by the Kindergarten supply houses. Clay modeling gives the child even more joy than sand modeling, because objects made of clay may be moved about and kept as long as desired, while the sandhouse or sheep fold falls into nothingness if the table is jarred. It is surprising how deftly even the smallest children learn to work with clay, and how clearly they will express their ideas through this medium. To my notion it is the most satisfactory form of hand work to use in connection with the story. Cutting and drawing require more skill than modeling, and the child can tell with clay what he cannot say with scissors and pencil.

Here also questioning and suggestion should call

into play the child's creative impulses and make him feel that he wants to express something. Do not say, "Now go to the table and see what you can make." Say instead, "Who can make the hills where David pastured the sheep and the streams where they drank?" Such questioning creates a definite picture in the mind and the modeling will be an expression of that picture.

Retelling the story.—Another specific use of the story is retelling it by the child, by a group of children, or by the children aided by the teacher, she to begin unwinding the plot thread and they to carry it on to completion. In this way no one child monopolizes the tale, as frequently happens when no effort is made to make the retelling a piece of class work. It gives the shy child an equal chance with the forward one, and, moreover, beginning the story by the teacher removes the difficulty so often experienced by the child who does not know what to say first. Beginning a tale, even for an adult, is more difficult than unwinding the plot thread once the characters are introduced, and this explains why it happens that so often children who are thoroughly familiar with a story sit unresponsive to the question, "Who will tell it to me?" But with the characters in action they experience no difficulty in telling what they do next.

Retelling the tale is the most difficult of the several forms of story expression for the child, because it involves a complicated thought process, visualizing of scenes and word control at the same time. It should follow rather than precede the simpler forms of expression, such as pantomime dramatization, modeling, and singing the story. The teacher of beginners will find occasion to use it much less frequently than the other forms, perhaps not at all, unless she has in her group one or more gifted children who want to tell the story. The worker in the Primary Department will find more occasion to use it, but it is not until the children reach the junior age that the class as a whole will enjoy this form of expression.

Thus, through hearing a story, playing, singing, drawing, cutting, coloring or modeling it, the incidents that make its plot become a part of the child's own experience, its lessons laws that function in his code of action. Because of story experiences he learns to think more clearly, to feel more deeply, to live more richly and completely. In a word, he will be a better child to-day and a better man to-morrow than he can be without these experiences, and he will give to a succeeding generation according to the measure in which he has received. The germination process of the seed is hidden under the ground and the expanding emotional nature is not revealed to the eye. But while the boy listens, while he works out the story in any of the ways dear to childhood, he is learning and growing, and the fruit of that growth will be manifested some day in constructive action and beneficent living, even though she who sowed the seed may never see the rare coloring or inhale the fragrance of the flower.

THOUGHT QUESTIONS

1. What is the value of the child's expression of a story?

2. Why should the pantomime form of dramatization precede the oral form?

3. What danger lies in drawing, coloring, and paper cutting in the Sunday school? How may this danger be eliminated and these forms of handwork be made valuable?

4. Why is it advisable for the teacher to begin the story when the children are to retell it?

ASSIGNMENT

Prepare for telling the story of the Baby Moses. Exodus 2. 1-10.

Write questions and suggestions that will lead children to play it.

Write suggestions to the children for a song about the basket in the rushes.

Write suggestions that will lead the children to try to draw, cut or model the basket, the river bank, and the baby's home to which the mother took him.